BOB DYLAN THE LYRICS 1961—2020

SLOW TRAIN COMING

慢车开来

鲍勃 · 迪伦诗歌集 1961—2020

VOL.07

[美] 鲍勃 · 迪伦 著　李皖 译

中信出版集团 | 北京

合法上路

STREET LEGAL

附加歌词

慢车开来

SLOW TRAIN COMING

得救

SAVED

来一针爱

SHOT OF LOVE

附加歌词

STREET LEGAL
合法上路

守卫换岗

新的小马

宝贝，别哭

你的爱徒劳无益?

先生（扬基·鲍尔的故事）

真爱倾向于忘记

我们最好谈谈

今夜你在哪里?（穿越黑热之旅）

附加歌词

退伍军人病

Midwives stroll between jupiter & apollo
Struggling babes past (Between the sheets of...
A messenger arrives with a blck nightengale
I see her on the square & I cannot help but follow
Follow her down to the fountain where she's lifting her veil

she said, can y spare me a moment's passion
Can I shine yr shoes, print yr money or mark yr cards
What frozen truths can yr brave souls imagine
Does yr hearts have the courage for the changing of the guards

迪伦第18张录音室专辑，叫《合法上路》，由哥伦比亚唱片公司于1978年6月15日发行。“合法上路”是什么意思？为什么取这么个怪名？原来，这个名词指改装车验收合格、证照齐备，被允许在城市道路上行驶。评论家们认为，迪伦以此暗示离婚官司打完了，从此无纠缠一身轻。

无纠缠一身轻吗？可能正相反，它恰恰反映了迪伦深陷于这一段困境的状态。离婚官司打完了，他还是念念不忘，还要故作潇洒，把奇怪的“轻松”姿态投射到专辑命名和封面设计上。

1977年6月29日，迪伦与萨拉数年来的关系不和走到了终点，二人离婚。整个上半年，迪伦都深陷在离婚案中。眼见尘埃落定、春去夏来，他回到故乡明尼苏达州的农场，孩子们和新的恋爱对象法里迪·麦克弗里（Faridi McFree）陪伴着他。他开始创作新歌，《合法上路》中的9首歌曲，至少有6首是在这期间完成的。

8月16日，“猫王”埃尔维斯·普雷斯利（Elvis Presley）去世的消息传来，迪伦的工作被打乱了。后来，他在谈到这段时期的个人心境时说：“我回顾了我的一生，回顾了我的整个童年，有一个星期没和人说话。”

是年秋末冬初，迪伦在加州圣莫尼卡市租了一栋“破败”的两层老建筑，改造成排练场和录音室，筹划进行世界巡演。一些乐手接到邀请，于12月初抵达。但子女监护权之争让迪伦再次陷了进去，乐手们直到一两个星期后，才第一次见到迪伦。据乐手罗布·斯通纳（Rob Stoner）回忆，迪伦心烦意乱，一根接一根抽烟，完全没办法工作。

12月底，诉讼走到了终点，迪伦得到部分监护权，但这场争夺撕扯之激烈，使迪伦和萨拉好几年都无法和解。乐队开始排练，但迪伦的心境完全变了，《渴望》时期形成并得到他肯定的风格，完全被他放弃。他想要南方节奏布鲁斯（R&B），想要摩城（Motown）黑人灵魂乐，想要亲近“猫王”的音乐秀风格。

于是，乐队大换血。4月1日世界巡演结束，斯通纳请辞，乐队再次变动。迪伦组织了三人的女子福音伴唱，组建了包含2支萨克斯管的大型流行摇滚乐队，并在1978年4月25—28日，用4场录音，录制了9首作品。5月1—3日，迪伦又加了2场叠录。

如同女声福音合唱所暗示的，《合法上路》中最令人瞩目的，是那种仿佛天启式的写作。《守卫换岗》来自1976年的长诗《重新观察》（“An Observation Revisited”），迪伦说它“已经在迷雾中存在了好几千年，有一天我进入了它”。这首歌释放了迪伦要改变信仰的信号，好像从婚姻的灰烬中获得了反省和力量，他要“重生”了。

另一首天启式作品《先生（扬基·鲍尔的故事）》，通篇借用了《圣经》的概念。回忆和怀疑笼罩了他，这一条爱情之路，也是人生之路，终究又是人世之路，旅途漫漫，凶兆丛生，似乎通向人类末日。

《宝贝，别哭》《你的爱徒劳无益？》《真爱倾向于忘记》《我们最好谈谈》都是关于这场失败婚姻的扭曲镜像。我们如果把它们当作迪伦和萨拉的情事来看，应该能挖出很多八卦，却也显示出迪伦的偏执狭隘和自我美化；如果跳出现实世界，把它们当作艺术品来看，当作超越了具体人事的情歌来看，其卓异和优秀便显现出来。由于它们牵连着伤口、血肉、心灵，不是虚幻浪漫的商业假情歌，每个字背后都有真实的疼痛；由于它们来自一场撕扯了情感、亲缘、利益乃至精神的离异诉讼，这些歌曲描摹了深度罕见的人性，令人备感痛苦。

《新的小马》和《今夜你在哪里？（穿越黑热之旅）》都是双重隐喻，一场婚姻之旅也是一场信仰之途。源自布鲁斯文体的《新的小马》，带着美国黑人诗歌的印记，粗朴、诙谐而轻巧，但它也具有布鲁斯从没有过的宗教探索格局。《今夜你在哪里？（穿越黑热之旅）》的沉重达到了全专辑之最，迪伦在此倾泻了他对这场失败婚姻的所有负面感情。但迪伦的独特之处在于，他的心灵在此婚变中的感知是壮阔的，没有谁像他这样，会把一首爱情失败歌曲，唱成了人间、地狱和天堂之歌，竟似覆盖了他这一段时间所有的人生经历、内心经历和宗教体验经历。

CHANGING OF THE GUARDS

Sixteen years
Sixteen banners united over the field
Where the good shepherd grieves
Desperate men, desperate women divided
Spreading their wings 'neath the falling leaves

Fortune calls
I stepped forth from the shadows, to the marketplace
Merchants and thieves, hungry for power, my last deal gone down
She's smelling sweet like the meadows where she was born
On midsummer's eve, near the tower

The cold-blooded moon
The captain waits above the celebration
Sending his thoughts to a beloved maid
Whose ebony face is beyond communication
The captain is down but still believing that his love will be repaid

They shaved her head
She was torn between Jupiter and Apollo

守卫换岗

十六年
十六面旗帜联合飘扬
在好牧人哀悼的田野
绝望的男人、绝望的女人分离
在落叶下展开双翼

命运在召唤
我从阴影中举步向前，走向集市
生意人和贼，渴望权力，我最后一笔
　交易告吹
她身上的香气甜美得就像她降生的草地
在仲夏夜，高塔边

冷血之月
船长在庆典上空守望
将思念发送给他心爱的侍女
但毫无信息透出她黑檀木的面庞
船长很失落却仍相信他的爱必有
　回音

他们剃去了她一头青丝
她在朱庇特和阿波罗之间踌躇

A messenger arrived with a black nightingale
I seen her on the stairs and I couldn't help but follow
Follow her down past the fountain where they lifted her veil

I stumbled to my feet
I rode past destruction in the ditches
With the stitches still mending 'neath a heart-shaped tattoo
Renegade priests and treacherous young witches
Were handing out the flowers that I'd given to you

The palace of mirrors
Where dog soldiers are reflected
The endless road and the wailing of chimes
The empty rooms where her memory is protected
Where the angels' voices whisper to the souls of previous times

She wakes him up
Forty-eight hours later, the sun is breaking
Near broken chains, mountain laurel and rolling rocks
She's begging to know what measures he now will be taking
He's pulling her down and she's clutching on to his long golden
locks

信使带黑色夜莺来了
我在楼梯看见她，忍不住跟上去
跟着她越过了喷泉，在那里他们将她的面纱掀起

我两脚跌跌撞撞
跨过了沟渠里的毁灭
心形文身下的缝线仍在修补
叛变的神父和奸诈的年轻女巫
在分发我送给你的花朵

镜子大厅
倒映着犬兵[1]
无尽的路和钟的悲泣
保护着她记忆的空房间中
天使之声在对旧时代的灵魂低语

她叫醒了他
四十八小时后，太阳乍现
在砸断的锁链、山月桂和滚石边
她恳求他告知接下来的行动
他把她拉下来，她紧紧拽住他长长的
　金色发卷

---

[1] 犬兵，美国印第安夏延族部落的战士组织，夏延人迷信狗会转生为勇士，故名。

Gentlemen, he said
I don't need your organization, I've shined your shoes
I've moved your mountains and marked your cards
But Eden is burning, either brace yourself for elimination
Or else your hearts must have the courage for the changing of
the guards

Peace will come
With tranquillity and splendor on the wheels of fire
But will bring us no reward when her false idols fall
And cruel death surrenders with its pale ghost retreating
Between the King and the Queen of Swords

先生们，他说
我不需要你们的组织，我已经擦亮你们的鞋
移动了你们的山并标记了你们的卡片
但是伊甸园着火了，要么准备好被淘汰
要么你们的心一定要有守卫换岗的
　勇气

和平将到来
伴随着火轮的宁静与绚烂
但是和平不会给我们回报，当她的假偶倒下
而残酷的死亡投降，它苍白的幽灵
退到了宝剑国王和宝剑皇后[1]之间

[1] 宝剑国王和宝剑皇后，塔罗牌的两个牌面。

NEW PONY

Once I had a pony, her name was Lucifer
I had a pony, her name was Lucifer
She broke her leg and she needed shooting
I swear it hurt me more than it could ever have hurted her

Sometimes I wonder what's going on in the mind of Miss X
Sometimes I wonder what's going on in the mind of Miss X
You know she got such a sweet disposition
I never know what the poor girl's gonna do to me next

I got a new pony, she knows how to fox-trot, lope and pace
Well, I got a new pony, she knows how to fox-trot, lope and pace
She got great big hind legs
And long black shaggy hair above her face

Well now, it was early in the mornin', I seen your shadow in the door
It was early in the mornin', I seen your shadow in the door
Now, I don't have to ask nobody

新的小马

曾经我有一匹小马，名字叫路西法[1]
我有一匹小马，名字叫路西法
她的腿断了，她需要一枪
我发誓我的痛超过了她可能在承受的

有时我会猜 X 小姐脑子里在想什么
有时我会猜 X 小姐脑子里在想什么
你知道她性情这么美
我永远猜不到这可怜姑娘下一步怎么待我

我有了一匹新的小马，她会狐步、轻跳和溜蹄
是的，我有了一匹新的小马，她会狐步、轻跳和
　溜蹄
她有非常棒的后腿
脸上的鬃毛乱蓬蓬又长又黑

好吧，那是大清早，我看见你在门里的
　影子
那是大清早，我看见你在门里的影子
喏，我用不着问谁

---

[1] 路西法，明亮之星，即金星。后成为撒旦的代名词。

I know what you come here for

They say you're usin' voodoo, your feet walk by themselves
They say you're usin' voodoo, I seen your feet walk by
themselves
Oh, baby, that god you been prayin' to
Is gonna give ya back what you're wishin' on someone else

Come over here pony, I, I wanna climb up one time on you
Come over here pony, I, I wanna climb up one time on you
Well, you're so bad and nasty
But I love you, yes I do

我知道你来是为了什么

他们说你在使巫术，你的脚自动在走
他们说你在使巫术，我看到你的脚
　自动在走
啊，宝贝，你一直祈祷的那个神
会把你许给别人的愿回向给你

到这儿来小马，我，我想再一次爬上去
到这儿来小马，我，我想再一次爬上去
好吧，你是这么坏又难对付
但是我爱你，是的我爱你

BABY, STOP CRYING

You been down to the bottom with a bad man, babe
But you're back where you belong
Go get me my pistol, babe
Honey, I can't tell right from wrong

Baby, please stop crying, stop crying, stop crying
Baby, please stop crying, stop crying, stop crying
Baby, please stop crying
You know, I know, the sun will always shine
So baby, please stop crying 'cause it's tearing up my mind

Go down to the river, babe
Honey, I will meet you there
Go down to the river, babe
Honey, I will pay your fare

Baby, please stop crying, stop crying, stop crying
Baby, please stop crying, stop crying, stop crying
Baby, please stop crying
You know, I know, the sun will always shine
So baby, please stop crying 'cause it's tearing up my mind

宝贝，别哭

你和坏人一起落入谷底，宝贝
但是你回到了属于你的地方
去把我的手枪拿来，宝贝
亲爱的，我已辨不清是与非

宝贝，请别哭，别哭，别哭
宝贝，请别哭，别哭，别哭
宝贝，请别哭
你知道，我知道，太阳会永远照耀
所以宝贝，请别哭了，因为这会撕碎我的心

到河边去吧，宝贝
亲爱的，我们在那儿相会
到河边去吧，宝贝
亲爱的，我来付你的路费

宝贝，请别哭，别哭，别哭
宝贝，请别哭，别哭，别哭
宝贝，请别哭
你知道，我知道，太阳会永远照耀
所以宝贝，请别哭了，因为这会撕碎我的心

If you're looking for assistance, babe
Or if you just want some company
Or if you just want a friend you can talk to
Honey, come and see about me

Baby, please stop crying, stop crying, stop crying
Baby, please stop crying, stop crying, stop crying
Baby, please stop crying
You know, I know, the sun will always shine
So baby, please stop crying 'cause it's tearing up my mind

You been hurt so many times
And I know what you're thinking of
Well, I don't have to be no doctor, babe
To see that you're madly in love

Baby, please stop crying, stop crying, stop crying
Baby, please stop crying, stop crying, stop crying
Baby, please stop crying
You know, I know, the sun will always shine
So baby, please stop crying 'cause it's tearing up my mind

如果你想要找个帮手，宝贝
或者你只是要有人相陪
或者你只想有个能说话的朋友
亲爱的，过来看看我吧

宝贝，请别哭，别哭，别哭
宝贝，请别哭，别哭，别哭
宝贝，请别哭
你知道，我知道，太阳会永远照耀
所以宝贝，请别哭了，因为这会撕碎我的心

你被伤过许多回
所以我知道你在想什么
哦，我不必是医生，宝贝
也看得出你在疯狂地爱着

宝贝，请别哭，别哭，别哭
宝贝，请别哭，别哭，别哭
宝贝，请别哭
你知道，我知道，太阳会永远照耀
所以宝贝，请别哭了，因为这会撕碎我的心

IS YOUR LOVE IN VAIN?

Do you love me, or are you just extending goodwill?
Do you need me half as bad as you say, or are you just feeling
guilt?
I've been burned before and I know the score
So you won't hear me complain
Will I be able to count on you
Or is your love in vain?

Are you so fast that you cannot see that I must have solitude?
When I am in the darkness, why do you intrude?
Do you know my world, do you know my kind
Or must I explain?
Will you let me be myself
Or is your love in vain?

Well I've been to the mountain and I've been in the wind
I've been in and out of happiness
I have dined with kings, I've been offered wings
And I've never been too impressed

All right, I'll take a chance, I will fall in love with you
If I'm a fool you can have the night, you can have the morning

你的爱徒劳无益？

你是爱我，还是不过在发善心？
你需要我的程度有没有你说的一半，或只是
　你心中有愧？
我被灼伤过，我心里有数
所以你不会听到我抱怨
我是能指望你
还是你的爱就是徒劳无益？

你跑得太快因而看不见我孤独吗？
当我身处黑暗，为什么你要闯入呢？
你是懂我的世界，懂我的天性
还是需要我解释？
你是让我做自己
还是你的爱就是徒劳无益？

是的，我上过高山也曾置身风里
幸福我得到过也失去过
我曾与国王共进晚餐，有人曾给过我翅膀
我从不认为这有多了不起

好吧，冒个险，我爱上你
就当我是白痴，你将拥有我的夜，也拥有

too

Can you cook and sew, make flowers grow

Do you understand my pain?

Are you willing to risk it all

Or is your love in vain?

早晨

你会做饭缝衣，会养花吗?

你懂我的痛苦吗?

你是愿意赌上一切

还是你的爱就是徒劳无益?

SEÑOR
(TALES OF YANKEE POWER)

Señor, señor, do you know where we're headin'?
Lincoln County Road or Armageddon?
Seems like I been down this way before
Is there any truth in that, señor?

Señor, señor, do you know where she is hidin'?
How long are we gonna be ridin'?
How long must I keep my eyes glued to the door?
Will there be any comfort there, señor?

There's a wicked wind still blowin' on that upper deck
There's an iron cross still hanging down from around her neck
There's a marchin' band still playin' in that vacant lot
Where she held me in her arms one time and said, "Forget me
  not"

先生[1]
（扬基·鲍尔的故事）

先生，先生，你知道我们这是去哪里？
林肯县道[2]还是哈米吉多顿[3]？
好像这条路我以前走过
不知这么说对不对，先生？

先生，先生，你知道她藏在哪里吗？
我们还要骑行多久？
我还要盯着那扇门多久？
那里面会有安慰吗，先生？

恶风还在上甲板吹着
铁十字仍挂在她脖子上
军乐队还在空地吹打着
那一次她在那儿拥我入怀，说
“勿忘我”

---

[1] 本首诗中的“先生”均为西班牙语。

[2] 1878年，当时尚为准州的新墨西哥发生长达5个多月的“林肯县战争”，争取该县的政治和经济控制权，后演变成反抗法律和秩序的腐败与贪婪之战。

[3] 哈米吉多顿，末日大决战的战场。

Señor, señor, I can see that painted wagon
I can smell the tail of the dragon
Can't stand the suspense anymore
Can you tell me who to contact here, señor?

Well, the last thing I remember before I stripped and kneeled
Was that trainload of fools bogged down in a magnetic field
A gypsy with a broken flag and a flashing ring
Said, "Son, this ain't a dream no more, it's the real thing"

Señor, señor, you know their hearts is as hard as leather
Well, give me a minute, let me get it together
I just gotta pick myself up off the floor
I'm ready when you are, señor

Señor, señor, let's disconnect these cables
Overturn these tables
This place don't make sense to me no more
Can you tell me what we're waiting for, señor?

先生，先生，我能看见那辆油漆马车
我能闻见那龙尾巴的味道
再也受不了这份猜疑
能告诉我这儿联系谁吗，先生？

好吧，我在脱光跪下前最后记得的事
是这一火车的蠢货都陷进了磁场
一个吉卜赛人举着破旗，戴着闪光的戒指
说：“小子，这不再是梦，这是真的”

先生，先生，你知道他们的心硬得像皮革
好吧，给我一分钟，让我收拾收拾
我得自己从地上爬起来
你准备好了我也就好了，先生

先生，先生，让我们断开这些电缆
掀翻这些桌子
这地方对我来说没意义了
你能告诉我我们在等什么吗，先生？

TRUE LOVE TENDS TO FORGET

I'm getting weary looking in my baby's eyes
When she's near me she's so hard to recognize
I finally realize there's no room for regret
True love, true love, true love tends to forget

Hold me, baby be near
You told me that you'd be sincere
Every day of the year's like playin' Russian roulette
True love, true love, true love tends to forget

I was lyin' down in the reeds without any oxygen
I saw you in the wilderness among the men
Saw you drift into infinity and come back again
All you got to do is wait and I'll tell you when

You're a tearjerker, baby, but I'm under your spell
You're a hard worker, baby, and I know you well
But this weekend in hell is making me sweat
True love, true love, true love tends to forget

I was lyin' down in the reeds without any oxygen
I saw you in the wilderness among the men

真爱倾向于忘记

凝视着宝贝的眼我渐渐疲惫
我很难认出她当她挨我太近
我终于明白没有余地后悔
真爱，真爱，真爱倾向于忘记

抱着我宝贝，请贴紧
告诉我你是真心实意
今年的每一天都像玩俄罗斯轮盘赌
真爱，真爱，真爱倾向于忘记

我躺在芦苇丛中没了氧气
见你在荒原中身处人群里
见你飘入了无限又返回
你所要做的就是等待，我会告诉你何时

你是颗催泪弹，宝贝，但我中了你的咒语
你是个工作狂，宝贝，而我对你相当了解
但地狱中的这个周末让我汗流浃背
真爱，真爱，真爱倾向于忘记

我躺在芦苇丛中没了氧气
见你在荒原中身处人群里

Saw you drift into infinity and come back again
All you got to do is wait and I'll tell you when

You belong to me, baby, without any doubt
Don't forsake me, baby, don't sell me out
Don't keep me knockin' about from Mexico to Tibet
True love, true love, true love tends to forget

见你飘入了无限又返回
你所要做的就是等待，我会告诉你何时

你是我的，宝贝，确定无疑
别背叛我，宝贝，别出卖我
别让我在墨西哥和西藏间奔波
真爱，真爱，真爱倾向于忘记

WE BETTER TALK THIS OVER

I think we better talk this over
Maybe when we both get sober
You'll understand I'm only a man
Doin' the best that I can

This situation can only get rougher
Why should we needlessly suffer?
Let's call it a day, go our own different ways
Before we decay

You don't have to be afraid of looking into my face
We've done nothing to each other time will not erase

I feel displaced, I got a low-down feeling
You been two-faced, you been double-dealing
I took a chance, got caught in the trance
Of a downhill dance

Oh, child, why you wanna hurt me?
I'm exiled, you can't convert me
I'm lost in the haze of your delicate ways
With both eyes glazed

我们最好谈谈

我想我们最好谈谈
也许等我们俩都清醒
你会明白我只是个人
尽了一己所能

这状况只会越来越糟
我们干吗要无谓受苦?
到此为止吧，各走各的路
趁着我们还没进坟墓

不必害怕看我的脸
我们彼此造下的，时间都会抹去

这让我不安，情绪压抑
你明一套暗一套，表里不一
我孤注一掷，却陷入了
摇摇晃晃走下坡路的恍惚

啊，孩子，为什么要伤害我?
我已经被流放，你不能再改我的信仰
迷失在你姿态曼妙的烟雾中
我的两眼一片迷蒙

You don't have to yearn for love, you don't have to be alone
Somewheres in this universe there's a place that you can call
home

I guess I'll be leaving tomorrow
If I have to beg, steal or borrow
It'd be great to cross paths in a day and a half
Look at each other and laugh

But I don't think it's liable to happen
Like the sound of one hand clappin'
The vows that we kept are now broken and swept
'Neath the bed where we slept

Don't think of me and fantasize on what we never had
Be grateful for what we've shared together and be glad
Why should we go on watching each other through a
telescope?
Eventually we'll hang ourselves on all this tangled rope

Oh, babe, time for a new transition
I wish I was a magician
I would wave a wand and tie back the bond
That we've both gone beyond

你不必渴望爱，你不必孤独
这宇宙中总有个地方，你可以
　叫作家

我想我明天就走
即使必须去偷、去借、去乞讨
能在一天半后不期而遇真是太好
彼此相视一笑

但我觉得这不可能发生
一个巴掌拍不出声音
我们的誓言今已破碎
被扫入我们曾共眠的床底

不要再想我了，也不要幻想如果了
感谢我们曾共享的，高兴起来吧
何必透过望远镜继续窥望
　彼此？
那只会让我们在乱麻中最终吊死

啊，宝贝，是重新转变的时候了
真希望我是个魔法师
挥一挥魔杖就又系上
那个被我们绷断的绳结

WHERE ARE YOU TONIGHT?
(JOURNEY THROUGH DARK HEAT)

There's a long-distance train rolling through the rain
Tears on the letter I write
There's a woman I long to touch and I miss her so much
But she's drifting like a satellite

There's a neon light ablaze in this green smoky haze
Laughter down on Elizabeth Street
And a lonesome bell tone in that valley of stone
Where she bathed in a stream of pure heat

Her father would emphasize you got to be more than streetwise
But he practiced what he preached from the heart
A full-blooded Cherokee, he predicted to me
The time and the place that the trouble would start

There's a babe in the arms of a woman in a rage
And a longtime golden-haired stripper onstage
And she winds back the clock and she turns back the page
Of a book that no one can write
Oh, where are you tonight?

今夜你在哪里？
（穿越黑热之旅）

有一列远途列车滚滚驰过雨幕
泪水打湿了我正在写的信
有一个女人我渴望着爱抚，我是多么想她
可是她在漂流仿佛是一颗卫星

有一盏霓虹灯在绿色烟雾中燃烧
欢笑声在伊丽莎白大街飘落
而石头谷有寂寥的钟
她在那儿沐浴，在纯净炽热的溪流中

她父亲强调你要超越街头智慧
而他的行事一如他发乎于心的说教
一个纯血统切罗基人，他向我预示着
麻烦将发生的时间和地点

有一个宝宝依偎在愤怒女人怀抱
这金发妹是舞台上的老牌脱衣舞女
她倒转时光，将一本没人写的书
翻回到那一页
啊，今夜你在哪里？

The truth was obscure, too profound and too pure
To live it you have to explode
In that last hour of need, we entirely agreed
Sacrifice was the code of the road

I left town at dawn, with Marcel and St. John
Strong men belittled by doubt
I couldn't tell her what my private thoughts were
But she had some way of finding them out

He took dead-center aim but he missed just the same
She was waiting, putting flowers on the shelf
She could feel my despair as I climbed up her hair
And discovered her invisible self

There's a lion in the road, there's a demon escaped
There's a million dreams gone, there's a landscape being raped
As her beauty fades and I watch her undrape
I won't but then again, maybe I might
Oh, if I could just find you tonight

I fought with my twin, that enemy within
'Til both of us fell by the way

真相扑朔迷离，太深邃也太纯粹
依此生活你必将崩溃
在最后的艰难时刻，我们完全同意
牺牲是这条路上的行为准则

黎明时，我和马塞尔[1]和圣约翰离开小镇
坚定的人，被怀疑者轻看
我无法告知她我的隐秘想法
但是她总有办法发现

他瞄准了正中心却偏离了正中心
她等待着，把花摆入架子
她能感到我的绝望，当我爬上她的秀发
结果发现了她看不见的自我

有一头狮子挡道，有一个魔鬼逃跑
有一百万个梦破灭，有一片风景被强暴
当她美色凋零，而我望着她解带宽衣
我不会但话说回来，也可能我会
啊，但愿我能在今夜找到你

我与我的孪生体，那内心的敌人搏斗
直到我们俩都倒在了半路

---

[1] 加布里埃尔·马塞尔（Gabriel Marcel，1889—1973），法国存在主义哲学家，1929年皈依天主教。

Horseplay and disease is killing me by degrees
While the law looks the other way

Your partners in crime hit me up for nickels and dimes
The guy you were lovin' couldn't stay clean
It felt outa place, my foot in his face
But he should-a stayed where his money was green

I bit into the root of forbidden fruit
With the juice running down my leg
Then I dealt with your boss, who'd never known about loss
And who always was too proud to beg

There's a white diamond gloom on the dark side of this room
And a pathway that leads up to the stars
If you don't believe there's a price for this sweet paradise
Remind me to show you the scars

There's a new day at dawn and I've finally arrived
If I'm there in the morning, baby, you'll know I've survived
I can't believe it, I can't believe I'm alive
But without you it just doesn't seem right
Oh, where are you tonight?

胡闹和疾病让我一点点死亡
而律法对此别过头去

你的同伙为了五分一毛钱对我穷追不舍
你爱的那伙计没办法保持干净
这感觉不对劲儿，我的脚在他脸上
而他本该待在钱是绿色的地方[1]

我咬进了禁果的根
汁液顺着腿往下流
然后我和你老板交易，他从不知道何谓失去
总是不肯屈尊俯就

有一束白钻石的忧郁在这房间暗处
也有一条小路一直通向星辰
如果你不信这美好天堂是有代价的
提醒我，我给你看那些伤痕

黎明那儿有新的一天，而我终于抵达
假如早晨我在那儿，宝贝，你可知我幸存
我简直不相信，不相信我还活着
但是没有了你总像是不对
啊，今夜你在哪里？

---

[1] 美元钞票为绿色，习语中称非法收益为黑钱（black money），这里反向用，应指合法收入。

LEGIONNAIRE'S DISEASE

Some say it was radiation, some say there was acid on the
  microphone
Some say a combination that turned their hearts to stone
But whatever it was, it drove them to their knees
Oh, Legionnaire's disease

I wish I had a dollar for everyone that died within that year
Got 'em hot by the collar, plenty an old maid shed a tear
Now within my heart, it sure put on a squeeze
Oh, that Legionnaire's disease

Granddad fought in a revolutionary war, father in the War of
  1812
Uncle fought in Vietnam and then he fought a war all by
  himself
But whatever it was, it came out of the trees
Oh, that Legionnaire's disease

退伍军人病[1]

有人说是辐射，有人说麦克风上
　有酸
有人说是一种结合体把他们的心石化了
但不管那是什么，它让他们双膝跪地
啊，退伍军人病

真希望我能给那年死掉的人每人一美元
揪住衣领让他们发热，让足够多的老姑娘泪水涟涟
现在我的心里，它一定引起了一阵紧缩
啊，那退伍军人病

祖父打了独立战争，父亲打了1812年
　战争
叔叔在越南打，然后又一个人打了一场
　战争
但不管那是什么，它来自那些丛林
啊，那退伍军人病

---

[1] 退伍军人病，由嗜肺军团菌感染引起的急性呼吸道炎症，因1976年美国费城退伍军人大会上首次暴发而得名。当时有221人发病，34人死亡。

SLOW TRAIN COMING

慢车开来

总得服务某人

珍贵的天使

我相信你

慢车

要改变我的思维方式

要改变我的思维方式（另一版本）

待我好，宝贝（一样地待他人）

人给所有动物取了名

当他归回

附加歌词

没有义人，连一个也没有

烦恼在心间

你将被改变

Suddenly I turned around, she was standing there
with silver bracelets on wrists and flowers in her hair
She walked up to me so gracefully and took my crown of thorns
"Come in" she said "I'll give you shelter from the storm"

《慢车开来》于1979年8月20日由哥伦比亚唱片公司发行，是迪伦的第19张录音室专辑，也是他皈依基督教后的第1张专辑。

1978年下半年，迪伦受到了职业生涯中最严厉的批评：关于他的新电影《雷纳尔多与克拉拉》(*Renaldo and Clara*)，关于他的专辑《合法上路》，关于他的最新巡回演出，铺天盖地都是差评。

自婚姻破裂以来，迪伦有时会为与妻儿的分离而痛苦。生活中，他的安宁感消失了，个人日常似乎缺乏目标感。巡演途中，在亚利桑那州的图森酒店，有一天晚上，迪伦确信自己在房间中经历了基督的异象。“耶稣确实以万王之王、万主之主的身份出现在我面前，”他后来说，“房间里有一个存在，不可能是任何人，只能是耶稣……耶稣把手放在我身上。这是身体上的东西。我感觉到了。我感觉到它遍布我全身。我感觉我的全身都在颤抖。主的荣耀击倒了我，又将我扶起。”[1]

---

[1] Heylin, Clinton (2003). *Bob Dylan: Behind the Shades Revisited*. Harper Collins. pp. 491–502.

1978年9月22日，在纽约州雪城演唱会上，迪伦以寥寥数语宣布皈依基督教。在巡演最后两周试音期间，他创作了歌曲《慢车》。最后一场，在佛罗里达州好莱坞的演出中，他演唱了新歌《待我好，宝贝（一样待他人）》，这是他围绕《圣经》格言写的第一首歌，歌名的这句话，实际上是耶稣说的。

迪伦一直是一个博览群书的人，以前《圣经》对他来说只是一个文学来源，但现在不是了，它成了白纸黑字写出来的预言——当前的世界事件，正在《圣经》已经写下的章节中演进。

《慢车开来》中的歌曲，包括录音过程中产生但没有收进专辑的歌曲，所有歌词都深受《圣经》影响。显然，信仰的转变给他带来了精神慰藉，也让他在作词作曲方面获得了灵感。比如，《当他归回》直接借鉴了《启示录》。现在，对世界末日将要到来的信念几乎反映在他创作的所有歌曲中。1984年，迪伦在接受采访时说："我为《慢车开来》专辑写的歌曲（令我害怕）……我没有打算写它……我不喜欢写它。我不想写它。"

专辑的制作集结了一批高手中的高手。曾为诸多黑人音乐巨匠制作歌曲的杰里·韦克斯勒（Jerry Wexler）担任制作人，吉他圣手马克·诺夫勒（Mark Knopfler）担任主音吉他手，录音地点则是美国最厉害的马斯尔·肖尔斯录音室（Muscle Shoals Sound Studio）。韦克斯勒与迪伦的录音方式不同，他先录节奏轨，再录人声。1979年4月30日至5月11日，以这种方式，迪伦与乐队录下了12首歌。与他之前的专辑进度不同，这次录音在缓慢的开局后，进入高效而顺畅的后半程，其中 10 首歌曲是在 3 天时间内、6 场录音中高速完成的。

专辑面世后，摇滚评论家给予了毫不留情的批评。其中，最尖锐的评论来自格雷尔·马库斯，他称迪伦在“推销别处所得的预先包装好的教条”。相似地，安·德鲁扬（Ann Druyan）则平实地指出这回迪伦的转变：“我一直深爱迪伦的一点是他隐喻的勇气，以及他能够深深切入某种赤裸裸感觉的方式。这总是显得非常够胆。然而现在，他看来已经转过身去，他被光蒙蔽了双眼，他在寻找似乎简单的解答。”

如查尔斯·沙尔·默里（Charles Shaar Murray）所指出的，“鲍勃·迪伦似乎从未像这张专辑那样完美、令人印象深刻，他也从未显得如此令人不快和充满仇恨”，这张专辑引起了两极评论——一方面，录音、演奏和演唱是如此精湛，歌声充满了激情和细节；另一方面，它的主题是如此刻板：歌曲要么表达个人信仰，要么宣讲基督教义。专辑的福音性质疏远了迪伦的许多歌迷；与此同时，许多基督徒成为他新的拥趸。

这一时期，迪伦拒绝在演唱会表演自己的旧作，尽管他的牧师肯定其旧作并不算是亵渎，但迪伦表示不会唱“任何不是主给我唱的歌”。

全专辑中，《慢车》这首歌值得特别留意，这是一首未直接引用《圣经》的歌曲。它将个人经历与社会图景以及时事评论熔于一炉，具有宽广的视野和圆融的杂糅性，标示了迪伦叙事诗写作的新水平。

GOTTA SERVE SOMEBODY

You may be an ambassador to England or France
You may like to gamble, you might like to dance
You may be the heavyweight champion of the world
You may be a socialite with a long string of pearls

But you're gonna have to serve somebody, yes indeed
You're gonna have to serve somebody
Well, it may be the devil or it may be the Lord
But you're gonna have to serve somebody

You might be a rock 'n' roll addict prancing on the stage
You might have drugs at your command, women in a cage
You may be a businessman or some high-degree thief
They may call you Doctor or they may call you Chief

But you're gonna have to serve somebody, yes indeed
You're gonna have to serve somebody
Well, it may be the devil or it may be the Lord
But you're gonna have to serve somebody

You may be a state trooper, you might be a young Turk
You may be the head of some big TV network

总得服务某人

你可能是驻英或驻法大使
你可能喜欢赌博，你可能喜欢跳舞
你可能是世界重量级拳王
你可能是名媛，戴着长长的珍珠项链

但你必须服务某人，是的没错
你必须服务某人
哦，他可能是魔，可能是主
但你必须服务某人

你可能是台上跳来跳去的摇滚迷
你可能掌握着毒品，女人关在笼子里
你可能是商人或一种高明小偷
他们可能叫你医生，或者他们可能叫你老总

但你必须服务某人，是的没错
你必须服务某人
哦，他可能是魔，可能是主
但你必须服务某人

你可能是州警，你可能是少壮派
你可能是某大型电视网的头儿

You may be rich or poor, you may be blind or lame
You may be living in another country under another name

But you're gonna have to serve somebody, yes indeed
You're gonna have to serve somebody
Well, it may be the devil or it may be the Lord
But you're gonna have to serve somebody

You may be a construction worker working on a home
You may be living in a mansion or you might live in a dome
You might own guns and you might even own tanks
You might be somebody's landlord, you might even own banks

But you're gonna have to serve somebody, yes indeed
You're gonna have to serve somebody
Well, it may be the devil or it may be the Lord
But you're gonna have to serve somebody

You may be a preacher with your spiritual pride
You may be a city councilman taking bribes on the side
You may be workin' in a barbershop, you may know how to cut hair
You may be somebody's mistress, may be somebody's heir

But you're gonna have to serve somebody, yes indeed
You're gonna have to serve somebody

你可能富有或贫穷，你可能失明或跛足
你可能住另一个国家，用另一个名字

但你必须服务某人，是的没错
你必须服务某人
哦，他可能是魔，可能是主
但你必须服务某人

你可能是在房顶干活的建筑工
你可能住豪宅，你可能住在穹窿下
你可能有枪，你甚至可能有坦克
你可能是某人的房东，你甚至可能有银行

但你必须服务某人，是的没错
你必须服务某人
哦，他可能是魔，可能是主
但你必须服务某人

你可能是传教士，有着属灵的骄傲
你可能是市议员，偷偷摸摸受贿
你可能在理发店工作，你可能懂如何
　剪头
你可能是某人的情妇，可能是某位继承人

但你必须服务某人，是的没错
你必须服务某人

Well, it may be the devil or it may be the Lord
But you're gonna have to serve somebody

Might like to wear cotton, might like to wear silk
Might like to drink whiskey, might like to drink milk
You might like to eat caviar, you might like to eat bread
You may be sleeping on the floor, sleeping in a king-sized bed

But you're gonna have to serve somebody, yes indeed
You're gonna have to serve somebody
Well, it may be the devil or it may be the Lord
But you're gonna have to serve somebody

You may call me Terry, you may call me Timmy
You may call me Bobby, you may call me Zimmy
You may call me R.J., you may call me Ray
You may call me anything but no matter what you say

You're gonna have to serve somebody, yes indeed
You're gonna have to serve somebody
Well, it may be the devil or it may be the Lord
But you're gonna have to serve somebody

哦，他可能是魔，可能是主
但你必须服务某人

可能喜欢穿棉布，可能喜欢穿丝绸
可能喜欢威士忌，可能喜欢喝牛奶
你可能喜欢鱼子酱，你可能喜欢吃面包
你可能睡地板，睡特大号床

但你必须服务某人，是的没错
你必须服务某人
哦，他可能是魔，可能是主
但你必须服务某人

你可以叫我特里，你可以叫我蒂米
你可以叫我鲍比，你可以叫我齐米
你可以叫我 R. J.，你可以叫我雷
你可以随便叫我，但不管你说什么

你必须服务某人，是的没错
你必须服务某人
哦，他可能是魔，可能是主
但你必须服务某人

PRECIOUS ANGEL

Precious angel, under the sun
How was I to know you'd be the one
To show me I was blinded, to show me I was gone
How weak was the foundation I was standing upon?

Now there's spiritual warfare and flesh and blood breaking
down
Ya either got faith or ya got unbelief and there ain't no neutral
ground
The enemy is subtle, how be it we are so deceived
When the truth's in our hearts and we still don't believe?

Shine your light, shine your light on me
Shine your light, shine your light on me
Shine your light, shine your light on me
Ya know I just couldn't make it by myself
I'm a little too blind to see

My so-called friends have fallen under a spell
They look me squarely in the eye and they say, "All is well"
Can they imagine the darkness that will fall from on high
When men will beg God to kill them and they won't be able to

珍贵的天使

珍贵的天使，日光之下
我怎么知道你就是那位
昭示我被蒙蔽，昭示我无药可医
而我脚下的根基又是那么虚弱？

眼下正进行着属灵的对战，血肉
　分离
你要么有信仰要么不信，没有中立
　之地
敌人很狡猾，我们怎么就这样被骗
真相在我们心中，而我们依然不信？

照亮你的光，请为我照亮
照亮你的光，请为我照亮
照亮你的光，请为我照亮
你知道凭我一个人做不到
我有点儿瞎了，看不见了

我所谓的朋友都中了邪
他们直视着我的眼，他们说："一切都很好"
他们能想象黑暗将从天而降吗
当人求上帝杀死他们，他们却无法

die?

Sister, lemme tell you about a vision I saw
You were drawing water for your husband, you were suffering under the law
You were telling him about Buddha, you were telling him about Mohammed in the same breath
You never mentioned one time the Man who came and died a criminal's death

Shine your light, shine your light on me
Shine your light, shine your light on me
Shine your light, shine your light on me
Ya know I just couldn't make it by myself
I'm a little too blind to see

Precious angel, you believe me when I say
What God has given to us no man can take away
We are covered in blood, girl, you know our forefathers were slaves
Let us hope they've found mercy in their bone-filled graves

You're the queen of my flesh, girl, you're my woman, you're my delight

死去？

姐姐，让我告诉你我看到的异象
你在为你丈夫打水，你在律法之下
受苦
你跟他讲佛祖，同时跟他讲
穆罕默德
你一次也没提到那个人，他到来，以罪犯
之名死去[1]

照亮你的光，请为我照亮
照亮你的光，请为我照亮
照亮你的光，请为我照亮
你知道凭我一个人做不到
我有点儿瞎了，看不见了

珍贵的天使，你相信我，听我说
神赐予我们的，没有人能夺走
我们浑身是血，姑娘，你知道我们的
先祖是奴隶
让我们祈望他们在满是白骨的坟墓中找到了怜悯

你是我肉身的女王，姑娘，你是我的女人，你是
我的喜悦

---

[1] “你一次也没提到那个人，他到来，以罪犯之名死去”，指耶稣之死。

You're the lamp of my soul, girl, and you torch up the night
But there's violence in the eyes, girl, so let us not be enticed
On the way out of Egypt, through Ethiopia, to the judgment hall
of Christ

Shine your light, shine your light on me
Shine your light, shine your light on me
Shine your light, shine your light on me
Ya know I just couldn't make it by myself
I'm a little too blind to see

你是我灵魂的灯，姑娘，你点燃了黑夜
但那眼睛中有暴力，姑娘，所以让我们不被诱惑
在出埃及的路上，穿过埃塞俄比亚，前往基督的
　审判厅

照亮你的光，请为我照亮
照亮你的光，请为我照亮
照亮你的光，请为我照亮
你知道凭我一个人做不到
我有点儿瞎了，看不见了

I BELIEVE IN YOU

They ask me how I feel
And if my love is real
And how I know I'll make it through
And they, they look at me and frown
They'd like to drive me from this town
They don't want me around
'Cause I believe in you

They show me to the door
They say don't come back no more
'Cause I don't be like they'd like me to
And I walk out on my own
A thousand miles from home
But I don't feel alone
'Cause I believe in you

I believe in you even through the tears and the laughter
I believe in you even though we be apart
I believe in you even on the morning after
Oh, when the dawn is nearing
Oh, when the night is disappearing
Oh, this feeling is still here in my heart

我相信你

他们问我感觉如何
并且我的爱是不是真的
并且我怎么知道我会挺过去
并且他们，他们瞧着我皱起了眉头
他们想把我赶出镇子
他们不希望我在附近
因为我相信你

他们带我到门口
他们说别再回来了
因为我不是他们希望的样子
我独自走出去
离家一千里
但我不觉得孤单
因为我相信你

即使穿过泪水和嘲笑我也相信你
即使我们分开我也相信你
即使到第二天早上我还是相信你
啊，当黎明临近
啊，当夜色消失
啊，这感觉还在我心里

Don't let me drift too far
Keep me where you are
Where I will always be renewed
And that which you've given me today
Is worth more than I could pay
And no matter what they say
I believe in you

I believe in you when winter turn to summer
I believe in you when white turn to black
I believe in you even though I be outnumbered
Oh, though the earth may shake me
Oh, though my friends forsake me
Oh, even that couldn't make me go back

Don't let me change my heart
Keep me set apart
From all the plans they do pursue
And I, I don't mind the pain
Don't mind the driving rain
I know I will sustain
'Cause I believe in you

别让我漂离太远
让我留在你的所在
我将永获新生的所在
而你今天给我的
比我付得起的更值
所以不管他们说什么
我都相信你

当冬转为夏我相信你
当白变成黑我相信你
即使我寡不敌众我还是相信你
啊，尽管大地可能摇撼我
啊，虽然朋友们抛弃了我
啊，就算那样也不能让我回头

别让我改变心意
且让我远离
他们所追求的所有计划
而我，我不在意痛苦
不在意倾盆大雨
我知道我会坚持
因为我相信你

SLOW TRAIN

Sometimes I feel so low-down and disgusted
Can't help but wonder what's happenin' to my companions
Are they lost or are they found
Have they counted the cost it'll take to bring down
All their earthly principles they're gonna have to abandon?
There's a slow, slow train comin' up around the bend

I had a woman down in Alabama
She was a backwoods girl, but she sure was realistic
She said, "Boy, without a doubt
Have to quit your mess and straighten out
You could die down here, be just another accident statistic"
There's a slow, slow train comin' up around the bend

All that foreign oil controlling American soil
Look around you, it's just bound to make you embarrassed
Sheiks walkin' around like kings
Wearing fancy jewels and nose rings
Deciding America's future from Amsterdam and to Paris
And there's a slow, slow train comin' up around the bend

慢车 [1]

有时候觉得自己是这样卑微，令人厌恶
不禁想同伴们如今都怎么了
他们迷路了吧，他们醒悟了吧
他们有没有计算过，破坏那些原则的代价
那是些尘世的法则，最终将不得不全部抛弃
转过那弯道，一列缓慢、缓慢的火车，正在开来

我有一个女人，住在亚拉巴马
她是个林地姑娘，但是非常实际
她说："小子，毫无疑问
必须丢掉你的烂摊子，理清头绪
你会死在这儿，不过是又一个事故统计数字"
转过那弯道，一列缓慢、缓慢的火车，正在开来

外国石油控制着美国国土
瞧瞧你周围，就只会使你困窘
阿拉伯酋长像帝王一般四处走动
戴着华贵的珠宝和鼻环
从阿姆斯特丹到巴黎，决定着美国的命运
转过那弯道，一列缓慢、缓慢的火车，正在开来

---

[1] 本篇由郝佳校译。

Man's ego is inflated, his laws are outdated, they don't apply
no more
You can't rely no more to be standin' around waitin'
In the home of the brave
Jefferson turnin' over in his grave
Fools glorifying themselves, trying to manipulate Satan
And there's a slow, slow train comin' up around the bend

Big-time negotiators, false healers and woman haters
Masters of the bluff and masters of the proposition
But the enemy I see
Wears a cloak of decency
All nonbelievers and men stealers talkin' in the name of
religion
And there's a slow, slow train comin' up around the bend

People starving and thirsting, grain elevators are bursting
Oh, you know it costs more to store the food than it do to
give it
They say lose your inhibitions
Follow your own ambitions
They talk about a life of brotherly love show me someone who
knows how to live it
There's a slow, slow train comin' up around the bend

人类的自我恶性膨胀，他的律法已经过时，
　不再有效
你再不能站在那儿，只是等待
勇士的家乡
杰斐逊在坟墓里辗转反侧
愚人们在颂扬自己，试图操控撒旦
转过那弯道，一列缓慢、缓慢的火车，正在开来

大腕的谈判代表，造假的疗愈者和厌女者
装佯大师和企划大师
但是那敌人
我看见他身着庄重的披风
所有的不信者和抢人口的，全都以信仰的名义在
　高谈阔论
转过那弯道，一列缓慢、缓慢的火车，正在开来

人民饥饿干渴，谷仓却满得要爆炸
哦你应该知道，储存粮食比把它送出去
　更费钱
有人说放开你的压抑
服从你的野心
他们谈论着兄弟之爱，但请把知道如何这样生活的人
　指给我
转过那弯道，一列缓慢、缓慢的火车，正在开来

Well, my baby went to Illinois with some bad-talkin' boy she
could destroy
A real suicide case, but there was nothin' I could do to stop it
I don't care about economy
I don't care about astronomy
But it sure do bother me to see my loved ones turning into
puppets
There's a slow, slow train comin' up around the bend

唉，我的宝贝去了伊利诺伊，带着那位她能毁掉的
　脏话男孩
一桩真实的自杀事件，我却无法阻止，什么也做不了
我不关心经济
不关心天文学
但是眼看着我爱的人变成木偶，真的令我
　烦忧
转过那弯道，一列缓慢、缓慢的火车，正在开来

GONNA CHANGE MY WAY OF THINKING

Gonna change my way of thinking
Make myself a different set of rules
Gonna change my way of thinking
Make myself a different set of rules
Gonna put my good foot forward
And stop being influenced by fools

So much oppression
Can't keep track of it no more
So much oppression
Can't keep track of it no more
Sons becoming husbands to their mothers
And old men turning young daughters into whores

Stripes on your shoulders
Stripes on your back and on your hands
Stripes on your shoulders
Stripes on your back and on your hands
Swords piercing your side
Blood and water flowing through the land

Well don't know which one is worse

要改变我的思维方式

要改变我的思维方式
给自己定一套不同的规则
要改变我的思维方式
给自己定一套不同的规则
要向前迈出好的一步
不再受蠢货们影响

这么多的压迫
再无法找到踪迹
这么多的压迫
再无法找到踪迹
儿子成为母亲的丈夫
老父把年幼的女儿变成妓女

伤痕在你肩上
伤痕在你后背和手上
伤痕在你肩上
伤痕在你后背和手上
利剑刺入肋下
血和水流过大地

哦不知道哪个更糟

Doing your own thing or just being cool
Well don't know which one is worse
Doing your own thing or just being cool
You remember only about the brass ring
You forget all about the golden rule

You can mislead a man
You can take ahold of his heart with your eyes
You can mislead a man
You can take ahold of his heart with your eyes
But there's only one authority
And that's the authority on high

I got a God-fearing woman
One I can easily afford
I got a God-fearing woman
One I can easily afford
She can do the Georgia crawl
She can walk in the spirit of the Lord

Jesus said, "Be ready
For you know not the hour in which I come"

我行我素或只是冷酷
哦不知道哪个更糟
我行我素或只是冷酷
你只记得黄铜环[1]
全忘记了黄金律

你可以误导一个人
你可以用你的眼抓住他的心
你可以误导一个人
你可以用你的眼抓住他的心
但是权柄只有一个
那就是上天的权柄

我有个敬畏上帝的女人
我可以轻松负担得起
我有个敬畏上帝的女人
我可以轻松负担得起
她会跳佐治亚舞[2]
她会靠圣灵行事

耶稣说："做好准备
因为你不知道我来的时辰"

---

[1] 黄铜环，俚语指能致发迹、成功的机遇。骑旋转木马时，取得黄铜环可获得奖励。

[2] 佐治亚舞，20 世纪初一种布鲁斯舞蹈，舞姿多带性意味。

Jesus said, "Be ready
For you know not the hour in which I come"
He said, "He who is not for Me is against Me"
Just so you know where He's coming from

There's a kingdom called Heaven
A place where there is no pain of birth
There's a kingdom called Heaven
A place where there is no pain of birth
Well the Lord created it, mister
About the same time He made the earth

耶稣说：“做好准备
因为你不知道我来的时辰”
他说：“不与我相合的，就是敌我的”
因此你知道他会来自何处

有一个王国叫天国
一个无痛分娩之地
有一个王国叫天国
一个无痛分娩之地
哦主创造了它，先生
大约在同时，他创造了尘世

GONNA CHANGE MY WAY OF THINKING
(ALTERNATE VERSION)

Change my way of thinking, make myself a different set of rules
Change my way of thinking, make myself a different set of rules
Put my best foot forward, stop being influenced by fools

I'm sittin' at the welcome table, I'm so hungry I could eat a
horse
I'm sittin' at the welcome table, I'm so hungry I could eat a
horse
I'm gonna revitalize my thinking, I'm gonna let the law take its
course

Jesus is calling, He's coming back to gather up his jewels
Jesus is calling, He's coming back to gather up his jewels
We living by the golden rule, whoever got the gold rules

The sun is shining, ain't but one train on this track
The sun is shining, ain't but one train on this track
I'm stepping out of the dark woods, I'm jumping on the
monkey's back

I'm all dressed up, I'm going to the county dance

要改变我的思维方式

（另一版本）

改变我的思维方式，给自己定一套不同的规则
改变我的思维方式，给自己定一套不同的规则
向前迈出最好的一步，不再受蠢货们影响

我坐在迎宾席上，饿得能吃下
　一匹马
我坐在迎席宾上，饿得能吃下
　一匹马
我要重振我的思想，我要让那
　律法运行如常

耶稣在召唤，他要回来收拾他的珠玉
耶稣在召唤，他要回来收拾他的珠玉
我们都照黄金律生活，不管谁获得了黄金律

阳光朗照，这条轨道只有一列火车
阳光朗照，这条轨道只有一列火车
我走出黑暗森林，我跳上猴子
　后背

我已盛装打扮，要去参加县舞会

I'm all dressed up, I'm going to the county dance
Every day you got to pray for guidance
Every day you got to give yourself a chance

Storms are on the ocean, storms out on the mountain, too
Storms are on the ocean, storms out on the mountain, too
Oh Lord, you know I have no friend like you

I'll tell you something, things you never had you'll never miss
I'll tell you something, things you never had you'll never miss
A brave man will kill you with a sword, a coward with a kiss

我已盛装打扮，要去参加县舞会
每天你都要祈求指引
每天你都要给自己机会

海上有风暴，山上也有风暴
海上有风暴，山上也有风暴
啊我主，你知道我没有像你这样的朋友

我会告诉你一些事，这事你从未拥有永不会错过
我会告诉你一些事，这事你从未拥有永不会错过
勇士用剑取你性命，胆小鬼用吻

DO RIGHT TO ME BABY (DO UNTO OTHERS)

Don't wanna judge nobody, don't wanna be judged
Don't wanna touch nobody, don't wanna be touched
Don't wanna hurt nobody, don't wanna be hurt
Don't wanna treat nobody like they was dirt

But if you do right to me, baby
I'll do right to you, too
Ya got to do unto others
Like you'd have them, like you'd have them, do unto you

Don't wanna shoot nobody, don't wanna be shot
Don't wanna buy nobody, don't wanna be bought
Don't wanna bury nobody, don't wanna be buried
Don't wanna marry nobody if they're already married

But if you do right to me, baby
I'll do right to you, too
Ya got to do unto others
Like you'd have them, like you'd have them, do unto you

Don't wanna burn nobody, don't wanna be burned

待我好，宝贝
（一样地待他人）

不想评判任何人，不想被人评判
不想触碰任何人，不想被人触碰
不想伤害任何人，不想被人伤害
不想待任何人如同污秽

可是你若待我好，宝贝
我也会待你好
你要一样地待他人
就像你想要他们，就像你想要他们如何待你

不想枪击任何人，不想被人枪击
不想收买任何人，不想被人收买
不想埋葬任何人，不想被人埋葬
不想婚娶任何人，如果此人已婚

可是你若待我好，宝贝
我也会待你好
你要一样地待他人
就像你想要他们，就像你想要他们如何待你

不想烧死任何人，不想被人烧死

Don't wanna learn from nobody what I gotta unlearn
Don't wanna cheat nobody, don't wanna be cheated
Don't wanna defeat nobody if they already been defeated

But if you do right to me, baby
I'll do right to you, too
Ya got to do unto others
Like you'd have them, like you'd have them, do unto you

Don't wanna wink at nobody, don't wanna be winked at
Don't wanna be used by nobody for a doormat
Don't wanna confuse nobody, don't wanna be confused
Don't wanna amuse nobody, don't wanna be amused

But if you do right to me, baby
I'll do right to you, too
Ya got to do unto others
Like you'd have them, like you'd have them, do unto you

Don't wanna betray nobody, don't wanna be betrayed
Don't wanna play with nobody, don't wanna be waylaid
Don't wanna miss nobody, don't wanna be missed
Don't put my faith in nobody, not even a scientist

But if you do right to me, baby
I'll do right to you, too

不想向任何人学习必须摒弃的东西
不想欺骗任何人，不想被人欺骗
不想击败任何人，如果此人已经被击败

可是你若待我好，宝贝
我也会待你好
你要一样地待他人
就像你想要他们，就像你想要他们如何待你

不想对任何人挤眼，不想被人挤眼
不想被任何人用作擦鞋垫
不想迷惑任何人，不想被人迷惑
不想娱乐任何人，不想被人娱乐

可是你若待我好，宝贝
我也会待你好
你要一样地待他人
就像你想要他们，就像你想要他们如何待你

不想背叛任何人，不想被人背叛
不想游戏任何人，不想遭人伏击
不想怀念任何人，不想被人怀念
不要相信任何人，即使对科学家

可是你若待我好，宝贝
我也会待你好

Ya got to do unto others

Like you'd have them, like you'd have them, do unto you

你要一样地待他人

就像你想要他们，就像你想要他们如何待你

MAN GAVE NAMES TO ALL THE ANIMALS

Man gave names to all the animals
In the beginning, in the beginning
Man gave names to all the animals
In the beginning, long time ago

He saw an animal that liked to growl
Big furry paws and he liked to howl
Great big furry back and furry hair
"Ah, think I'll call it a bear"

Man gave names to all the animals
In the beginning, in the beginning
Man gave names to all the animals
In the beginning, long time ago

He saw an animal up on a hill
Chewing up so much grass until she was filled
He saw milk comin' out but he didn't know how
"Ah, think I'll call it a cow"

Man gave names to all the animals
In the beginning, in the beginning

人给所有动物取了名

人给所有动物取了名
在一开始，在一开始
人给所有动物取了名
在一开始，在很久以前

他看到一只动物喜欢咆哮
毛茸茸的大爪，而且他喜欢嚎叫
巨大的毛茸茸的背和毛茸茸的毛
“啊，我想我会叫它熊”

人给所有动物取了名
在一开始，在一开始
人给所有动物取了名
在一开始，在很久以前

他看到一只动物在山上
嚼那么多草她才终于吃饱
他看到奶出来了，但他不知道怎么出来的
“啊，我想我会叫它奶牛”

人给所有动物取了名
在一开始，在一开始

Man gave names to all the animals
In the beginning, long time ago

He saw an animal that liked to snort
Horns on his head and they weren't too short
It looked like there wasn't nothin' that he couldn't pull
"Ah, think I'll call it a bull"

Man gave names to all the animals
In the beginning, in the beginning
Man gave names to all the animals
In the beginning, long time ago

He saw an animal leavin' a muddy trail
Real dirty face and a curly tail
He wasn't too small and he wasn't too big
"Ah, think I'll call it a pig"

Man gave names to all the animals
In the beginning, in the beginning
Man gave names to all the animals
In the beginning, long time ago

Next animal that he did meet
Had wool on his back and hooves on his feet
Eating grass on a mountainside so steep

人给所有动物取了名
在一开始，在很久以前

他看到一只动物喜欢打喷嚏
它头上有角，而且还不算短
看来没什么是它拉不动的
“啊，我想我会叫它公牛”

人给所有动物取了名
在一开始，在一开始
人给所有动物取了名
在一开始，在很久以前

他看到一只动物留下一溜泥污
真正的脏脸和一条卷尾巴
他不太小也不太大
“啊，我想我会叫它猪”

人给所有动物取了名
在一开始，在一开始
人给所有动物取了名
在一开始，在很久以前

他遇到的下一个动物
背上有卷毛，脚上有蹄子
在这么陡的山腰上吃草

"Ah, think I'll call it a sheep"

Man gave names to all the animals
In the beginning, in the beginning
Man gave names to all the animals
In the beginning, long time ago

He saw an animal as smooth as glass
Slithering his way through the grass
Saw him disappear by a tree near a lake . . .

“啊，我想我会叫它羊”

人给所有动物取了名
在一开始，在一开始
人给所有动物取了名
在一开始，在很久以前

他看到一个动物光滑得像玻璃
滑行着穿过草丛
看到他消失在湖边一棵树旁……

WHEN HE RETURNS

The iron hand it ain't no match for the iron rod
The strongest wall will crumble and fall to a mighty God
For all those who have eyes and all those who have ears
It is only He who can reduce me to tears
Don't you cry and don't you die and don't you burn
For like a thief in the night, He'll replace wrong with right
When He returns

Truth is an arrow and the gate is narrow that it passes through
He unleashed His power at an unknown hour that no one knew
How long can I listen to the lies of prejudice?
How long can I stay drunk on fear out in the wilderness?
Can I cast it aside, all this loyalty and this pride?
Will I ever learn that there'll be no peace, that the war won't
cease
Until He returns?

Surrender your crown on this blood-stained ground, take off
your mask
He sees your deeds, He knows your needs even before you ask
How long can you falsify and deny what is real?
How long can you hate yourself for the weakness you conceal?

当他归回

铁手敌不过铁杖
最坚固的墙将在大能的神面前崩毁
对于所有生有眼和所有生有耳的人
唯有他会让我落泪
你不要哭，你不要死，你不要燃烧
因为就像夜间的贼，他会用对的换掉错的
当他归回

真理是一支箭，它穿过的是窄门
他释放他的力量，在所有人都不知晓的未知时辰
还有多久，我还要听这来自偏见的谎言？
还有多久，我还要因身处荒原的恐惧而迷醉？
所有这些忠诚和骄傲，我可以抛开吗？
将不会有和平，不会停止战争，一直到
　他归回
这一点我能否认清？

交出你的王冠吧，在这血迹斑斑的土地，摘下
　你的面具
他观你所为，他知你所需，甚至在你未开口时
还有多久，你还能歪曲和否认那些真实？
还有多久，你还能为你隐藏的弱点而厌憎自己？

Of every earthly plan that be known to man, He is
unconcerned
He's got plans of His own to set up His throne
When He returns

对于人类所知的每一个尘世计划，他都
　不感兴趣
他有他的计划，由此设立他的王位
当他归回

AIN'T NO MAN RIGHTEOUS, NO NOT ONE

When a man he serves the Lord, it makes his life worthwhile
It don't matter 'bout his position, it don't matter 'bout his lifestyle
Talk about perfection, I ain't never seen none
And there ain't no man righteous, no not one

Sometimes the devil likes to drive you from the neighborhood
He'll even work his ways through those whose intentions are good
Some like to worship on the moon, others are worshipping the sun
And there ain't no man righteous, no not one

Look around, ya see so many social hypocrites
Like to make rules for others while they do just the opposite

You can't get to glory by the raising and the lowering of no flag
Put your goodness next to God's and it comes out like a filthy rag
In a city of darkness there's no need of the sun
And there ain't no man righteous, no not one

没有义人，连一个也没有

一个人侍奉主，他的生命就有了价值
地位不重要，生活方式也
　不重要
说到完美无缺，我从来没见过
没有义人，连一个也没有

有时魔鬼喜欢将你从邻人那儿赶走
他甚至通过那些良善用心的人
　达成目的
有人喜欢膜拜月亮，其他人
　膜拜太阳
没有义人，连一个也没有

看看周围吧，你看这么多社会伪君子
喜欢为别人定规则，而自己恰恰相反行事

你不能通过升旗或降旗获得荣光
你的美德挨着上帝的美德，就会像一件
　肮脏的衣服
黑暗之城不需要太阳
没有义人，连一个也没有

Done so many evil things in the name of love, it's a crying
  shame
I never did see no fire that could put out a flame

Pull your hat down, baby, pull the wool down over your eyes
Keep a-talking, baby, 'til you run right out of alibis
Someday you'll account for all the deeds that you done
Well, there ain't no man righteous, no not one

God got the power, man has got his vanity
Man gotta choose before God can set him free
Don't you know there's nothing new that's under the sun?
Well, there ain't no man righteous, no not one

When I'm gone don't wonder where I be
Just say that I trusted in God and that Christ was in me
Say He defeated the devil, He was God's chosen Son
And that there ain't no man righteous, no not one

以爱为名犯下诸多恶事，真是
　奇耻大辱
我从未见过能扑灭火焰的火

把帽子拉低，宝贝，把眼睛遮住
继续扯，宝贝，直到用光借口
有朝一日你会对你做过的一切负责
嗯，没有义人，连一个也没有

上帝持有权柄，人持有虚荣
在上帝给他自由之前人须做出选择
难道你不知道日光之下并无新事？
嗯，没有义人，连一个也没有

当我离开尘世时，不要猜我在哪里
只说我信奉神，基督就在我心里
说他打败了魔鬼，他是上帝拣选之子
没有义人，连一个也没有

TROUBLE IN MIND

I got to know, Lord, when to pull back on the reins
Death can be the result of the most underrated pain
Satan whispers to ya, "Well, I don't want to bore ya
But when ya get tired of the Miss So-and-so I got another
   woman for ya"

Trouble in mind, Lord, trouble in mind
Lord, take away this trouble in mind

When the deeds that you do don't add up to zero
It's what's inside that counts, ask any war hero
You think you can hide but you're never alone
Ask Lot what he thought when his wife turned to stone

Trouble in mind, Lord, trouble in mind
Lord, take away this trouble in mind

Here comes Satan, prince of the power of the air
He's gonna make you a law unto yourself, gonna build a bird's
   nest in your hair
He's gonna deaden your conscience 'til you worship the work
   of your own hands

烦恼在心间

主啊，我必须知道何时收缰
死亡可能由最微不足道的疼痛导致
撒旦对着你耳语："嗯，我不想招你烦
但是，当你厌倦了某小姐，我给你另找个
　女人"

烦恼在心间，主啊，烦恼在心间
主啊，请将这心间的烦恼驱散

当你做下的事加起来不归零
作数的是内心的东西，问问任何一位战争英雄
你以为可以躲，可你从来都不是一个人
问问罗得，当妻子变成了石头，他怎么想

烦恼在心间，主啊，烦恼在心间
主啊，请将这心间的烦恼驱散

撒旦来了，空中掌权者的首领
他为你制定你自己的律法，在你的
　发丛中做窝
他让你良知昏睡，直到跪拜你自己
　手造的

You'll be serving strangers in a strange, forsaken land

Trouble in mind, Lord, trouble in mind
Lord, take away this trouble in mind

Well, your true love has caught you where you don't belong
You say, "Baby, everybody's doing it so I guess it can't be wrong"
The truth is far from you, so you know you got to lie
Then you're all the time defending what you can never justify

Trouble in mind, Lord, trouble in mind
Lord, take away this trouble in mind

So many of my brothers, they still want to be the boss
They can't relate to the Lord's kingdom, they can't relate to the cross
They self-inflict punishment on their own broken lives
Put their faith in their possessions, in their jobs or their wives

Trouble in mind, Lord, trouble in mind
Lord, take away this trouble in mind

When my life is over, it'll be like a puff of smoke
How long must I suffer, Lord, how long must I be provoked?
Satan will give you a little taste, then he'll move in with rapid

你将服侍外邦人，在陌生的、被遗弃的土地上

烦恼在心间，主啊，烦恼在心间
主啊，请将这心间的烦恼驱散

好吧，真爱抓住了你，在非你所属之地
你说："宝贝，人人如此，我料想
　这不会错"
真理离你很远，因此你知道必须撒谎
然后你就一直捍卫你永远无法证明的东西

烦恼在心间，主啊，烦恼在心间
主啊，请将这心间的烦恼驱散

我的那么多兄弟，他们仍想着做人上人
他们无法与主的王国关联，无法与十字架
　关联
他们对破碎的生命施以自我惩罚
将信仰寄托于财产，寄托于工作或自己的女人

烦恼在心间，主啊，烦恼在心间
主啊，请将这心间的烦恼驱散

当我的生命终结，它会像一团烟云
我要受苦多久，主啊，我要被刺激多久？
撒旦会给人点甜头，然后以飞快速度

speed

Lord, keep my blind side covered and see that I don't bleed

侵入

主啊，遮住我盲目的一侧，务使我不致流血

YE SHALL BE CHANGED

You harbor resentment
You know there ain't too much of a thrill
You wish for contentment
But you got an emptiness that can't be filled
You've had enough of hatred
Your bones are breaking, can't find nothing sacred

Ye shall be changed, ye shall be changed
In a twinkling of an eye, when the last trumpet blows
The dead will arise and burst out of your clothes
And ye shall be changed

Everything you've gotten
You've gotten by sweat, blood and muscle
From early in the morning 'til way past dark
All you ever do is hustle
All your loved ones have walked out the door
You're not even sure 'bout your wife and kids no more, but

Ye shall be changed, ye shall be changed
In a twinkling of an eye, when the last trumpet blows
The dead will arise and burst out of your clothes

你将被改变

你心怀怨愤
你知道没有太多刺激
你渴望满足
但你的空虚无法满足
你受够了仇恨
骨头在碎裂，找不到可神圣的

你将被改变，你将被改变
一眨眼间，末次号筒吹响死人复活
将绷开你的衣裳
你也要变样

你既得之种种
都凭着汗、血和肉获得
从大清早到天黑
你所做的就是忙忙碌碌
你爱的人全都出门离去
你甚至不很确定你的妻子孩子，但是

你将被改变，你将被改变
一眨眼间，末次号筒吹响
死人复活，将绷开你的衣裳

And ye shall be changed

The past don't control you
But the future's like a roulette wheel spinning
Deep down inside
You know you need a whole new beginning
Don't have to go to Russia or Iran
Just surrender to God and He'll move you right here where you
stand, and

Ye shall be changed, ye shall be changed
In a twinkling of an eye, when the last trumpet blows
The dead will arise and burst out of your clothes
And ye shall be changed

You drink bitter water
And you been eating the bread of sorrow
You can't live for today
When all you're ever thinking of is tomorrow
The path you've endured has been rough
When you've decided that you've had enough, then

Ye shall be changed, ye shall be changed
In a twinkling of an eye, when the last trumpet blows
The dead will arise and burst out of your clothes
And ye shall be changed

你也要变样

过去把控不了你
而未来像轮盘赌飞转
内心深处
你知道你需要一个全新起点
无须去俄罗斯或伊朗
只要归顺上帝，他就会从你站立处将你
　改变，而

你将被改变，你将被改变
一眨眼间，末次号筒吹响
死人复活，将绷开你的衣裳
你也要变样

你喝苦水
并且一直吃愁苦饭
你不能为今日活
而总是在思虑明日
你忍耐的路一直崎岖
而你决定不再忍受下去，那么

你将被改变，你将被改变
一眨眼间，末次号筒吹响
死人复活，将绷开你的衣裳
你也要变样

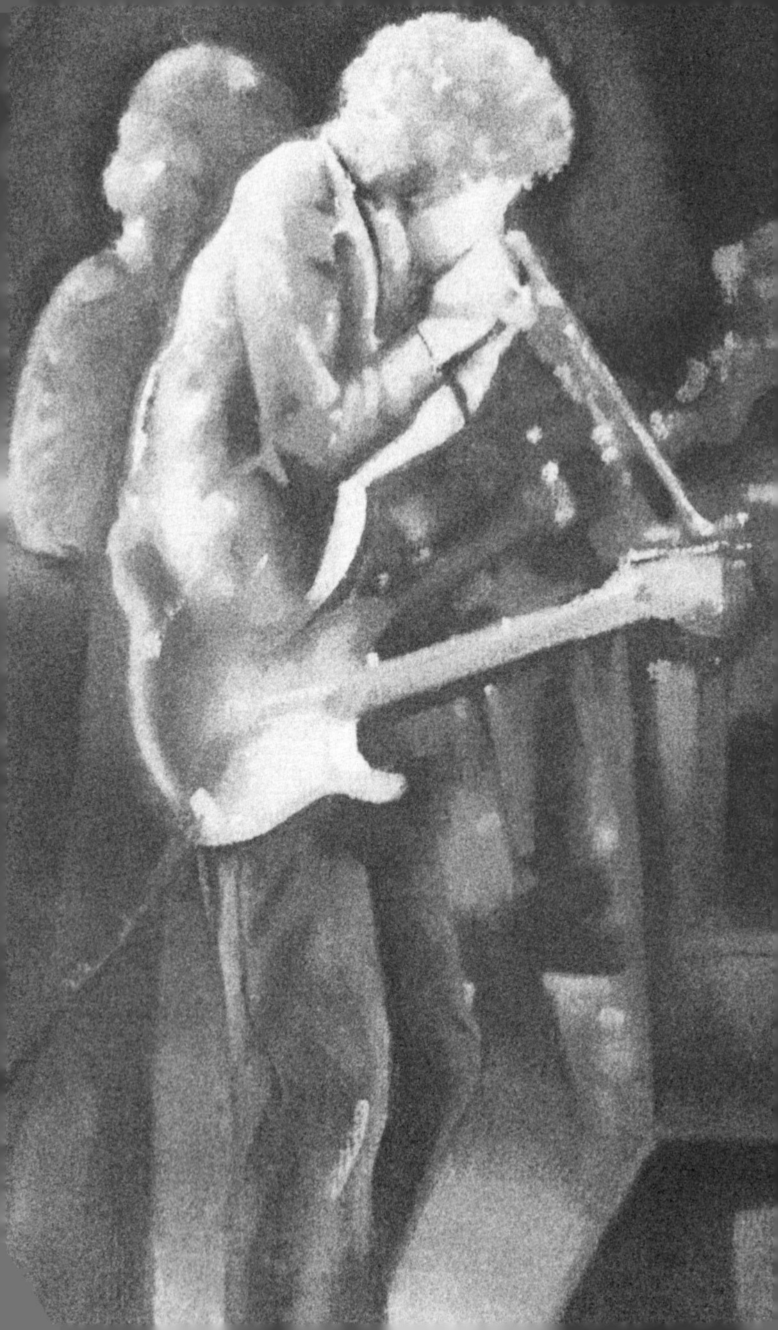

SAVED
得救

附加歌词

like a poor fool in his prime/trying to read your portrait
you can hear me talk

is your heart made of stone/
or solid rock?

1980 年 6 月 23 日，与《慢车开来》仅时隔 10 个月，哥伦比亚唱片公司发行了《得救》——迪伦的第 20 张录音室专辑。

这也是迪伦“基督教三部曲”的第 2 部，紧承《慢车开来》探索的主题，并将这一主题进一步聚焦于“信”与“恩”。

事实上，这些歌曲的写作在《慢车开来》录制一结束时就开始了。

1979 年 11 月 1 日起，迪伦在北美举办了 70 场演唱会，巡演从美国开到加拿大，一直到次年的 5 月 21 日才结束。人们在演唱会上看到了一个新迪伦——信奉耶稣基督的狂热信徒。每场表演前，乐队全体成员都会花一分钟时间在后台，彼此手拉手围成一个圈，然后有人会念一段《圣经》祷文。表演中，每次迪伦登场，都会拄着一根朝圣者的拐杖，他把巡演视为表达新信仰的一个机会。

这场历时半年多的巡演，迪伦不仅表演了《慢车开来》中的曲目，也表演了《得救》《立誓的女人》《我能为您做什么？》《坚固磐石》《奋力前进》《在园中》《救恩》等新的表达基督信念的作品。这都是在《慢车开来》录制结束后、巡演尚未开始前的短短两三个月中写的。

1980年2月11日，巡演尚未结束，迪伦即开始了新专辑的录音。制作人依然是杰里·韦克斯勒，录音地点仍然是在马斯尔·肖尔斯录音室。

大体上，《得救》专辑用带有狂喜色彩的福音编曲、昂扬向上的歌词，颂扬了迪伦坚定的个人信仰和他对基督深深的感恩之情。耶稣基督代他受过、为他开眼、给他救赎，恩情浩荡。同为信徒的著名制作人、歌曲作家“丁骨”伯内特（T Bone Burnett）说，皈依基督教后，“他（迪伦）感觉自己得救了，并为此兴奋不已”。

制作人韦克斯勒指出了《得救》与《慢车开来》的一个明显不同：“它的编曲已经成形了，乐队一直在现场表演这些歌。他们对大多数乐句了若指掌，巡演途中不断打磨完善。相反，上一张专辑里恐怖海峡乐队（Dire Straits）的精致伴奏，完完全全源于录音室。”

录音迅速而短暂，1980年2月11—15日，仅用了5天时间，整张专辑的录制即大功告成。

《得救》共有9首歌曲。除了非迪伦原创的开场曲《心满意足》（“A Satisfied Mind”），其他8首均收入这本诗集中。

这些歌曲，是迪伦对不断加深的信仰的公开告白。然而，值得注意的是，相形之下，它们并非标准的福音歌曲，而有着迪伦的个人心迹和个性特色，圣歌中有着自传的内容。《立誓的女人》完全就是迪伦的亲历记，讲对一个女人的爱，因她的爱而认识了上帝。《我能为您做什么？》，乍看与一般信徒心境相仿，若是细究，则有迪伦自己的心路历程。《坚固磐石》《奋力向前》讲信、讲心证，这确实是宗教信仰的两个核心；音乐形式上，这其实是摇滚歌曲。《在园中》无痕妙用布鲁斯的文体，将布鲁斯叠句化为无以复加的诘问语气——因而达到了在美学境界上难以企及的严厉。《准备好了吗？》尤其具有典型的迪伦式诗才——无比重大之事，以极简单的方式轻轻拿起，却直入核心；音乐上，它也不是福音歌曲，而是一首节奏咄咄逼人、气氛黑暗阴沉的布鲁斯。

《得救》专辑是迪伦最不被美国听众理解和认可的专辑之一，销量惨淡。评论界对这张专辑的反应褒贬不一。库尔特·洛德（Kurt Loder）指出，迪伦在福音专辑上的努力不像他的其他作为那样引人注目，“不仅因为他缺乏声乐设备，还因为对于这种音乐类型来说，他太有创造力，格局太大”。

这张专辑将迪伦带入了事业低谷。不仅评论家的反应显得犹疑不定，乐迷在不同时期对它的认识也飘飘忽忽。媒体总体上对它的评分极低，但2020年，《滚石》杂志将它列入了“1980年80张最伟大的专辑”榜单，称赞迪伦“正处于其声乐巅峰”。还有件事值得一提：直到2013年，迪伦还在演唱会上唱《准备好了吗？》，似乎宣示他并没有改弦更张，失去当初的信仰。

SAVED
(WITH TIM DRUMMOND)

I was blinded by the devil
Born already ruined
Stone-cold dead
As I stepped out of the womb
By His grace I have been touched
By His word I have been healed
By His hand I've been delivered
By His spirit I've been sealed

I've been saved
By the blood of the lamb
Saved
By the blood of the lamb
Saved
Saved
And I'm so glad
Yes, I'm so glad
I'm so glad
So glad
I want to thank You, Lord
I just want to thank You, Lord

得救

（与蒂姆·德拉蒙德合作）

我被魔鬼蒙蔽
出生时已毁
是冷如顽石的死人
走出了子宫
因着他的恩，我被感动了
因着他的话，我被疗治了
因着他的手，我被解救了
因着他的灵，我得了封印

我得救了
因着羔羊之血
得救了
因着羔羊之血
得救了
得救了
我是如此喜悦
是的，我是如此喜悦
我是如此喜悦
如此喜悦
我要感谢您，上主
我只想感谢您，上主

Thank You, Lord

By His truth I can be upright
By His strength I do endure
By His power I've been lifted
In His love I am secure
He bought me with a price
Freed me from the pit
Full of emptiness and wrath
And the fire that burns in it

I've been saved
By the blood of the lamb
Saved
By the blood of the lamb
Saved
Saved
And I'm so glad
Yes, I'm so glad
I'm so glad
So glad
I want to thank You, Lord
I just want to thank You, Lord
Thank You, Lord

Nobody to rescue me

谢谢您，上主

因着他的真理，我得以正直
因着他的神力，我能够忍耐
因着他的权柄，我获得升举
在他的爱中，我安全无虞
他用重价赎了我
把我从坑中救出来
那里充满了虚空和怒气
燃烧着熊熊烈火

我得救了
因着羔羊之血
得救了
因着羔羊之血
得救了
得救了
我是如此喜悦
是的，我是如此喜悦
我是如此喜悦
如此喜悦
我要感谢您，上主
我只想感谢您，上主
谢谢您，上主

没人来营救我

Nobody would dare
I was going down for the last time
But by His mercy I've been spared
Not by works
But by faith in Him who called
For so long I've been hindered
For so long I've been stalled

I've been saved
By the blood of the lamb
Saved
By the blood of the lamb
Saved
Saved
And I'm so glad
Yes, I'm so glad
I'm so glad
So glad
I want to thank You, Lord
I just want to thank You, Lord
Thank You, Lord

没有人敢
我最后一次坠落
却因着他的仁慈，得获幸免
不靠着行为
但因对他呼召的信心
已经太久我一直受阻
已经太久我一直停滞不前

我得救了
因着羔羊之血
得救了
因着羔羊之血
得救了
得救了
我是如此喜悦
是的，我是如此喜悦
我是如此喜悦
如此喜悦
我要感谢您，上主
我只想感谢您，上主
谢谢您，上主

COVENANT WOMAN

Covenant woman got a contract with the Lord
Way up yonder, great will be her reward
Covenant woman, shining like a morning star
I know I can trust you to stay where you are

And I just got to tell you
I do intend
To stay closer than any friend
I just got to thank you
Once again
For making your prayers known
Unto heaven for me
And to you, always, so grateful
I will forever be

I've been broken, shattered like an empty cup
I'm just waiting on the Lord to rebuild and fill me up
And I know He will do it 'cause He's faithful and He's true
He must have loved me so much to send me someone as fine

立誓的女人[1]

立誓的女人与上主立约
向上走，广大是她的回报
立誓的女人，闪耀如一颗晨星
我知道我可信你，留在你这儿

我只想对你说
我确实打算，离你
比任何朋友都更近
我只想感谢你
再一次
因你的祈祷
为我上达天庭
对你，始终，充满感激
我将永远感激

我已残破，碎裂如一只空杯
我只是在等上主重建并充满我
我知道他会这样，因他是诚信因他是真实
他必是爱我极深，才差遣来像你这样

[1] 通常认为，这首歌词是写给美国黑人演员玛丽·爱丽丝·阿特斯的，她与迪伦在 1979 年前后的恋情推动了迪伦信仰基督教。

as you

And I just got to tell you
I do intend
To stay closer than any friend
I just got to thank you
Once again
For making your prayers known
Unto heaven for me
And to you, always, so grateful
I will forever be

Covenant woman, intimate little girl
Who knows those most secret things of me that are hidden
from the world
You know we are strangers in a land we're passing through
I'll always be right by your side, I've got a covenant too

And I just got to tell you
I do intend
To stay closer than any friend
I just got to thank you
Once again
For making your prayers known
Unto heaven for me
And to you, always, so grateful
I will forever be

好的人

我只想对你说
我确实打算，离你
比任何朋友都更近
我只想感谢你
再一次
因你的祈祷
为我上达天庭
对你，始终，充满感激
我将永远感激

立誓的女人，亲密的小女孩
知晓我深藏于世的最深
秘密
你知道在经行的大地上我们都是异乡人
我会一直在你身边，我也立下了圣约

我只想对你说
我确实打算，离你
比任何朋友都更近
我只想感谢你
再一次
因你的祈祷
为我上达天庭
对你，始终，充满感激
我将永远感激

WHAT CAN I DO FOR YOU?

You have given everything to me
What can I do for You?
You have given me eyes to see
What can I do for You?

Pulled me out of bondage and You made me renewed inside
Filled up a hunger that had always been denied
Opened up a door no man can shut and You opened it up so
wide
And You've chosen me to be among the few
What can I do for You?

You have laid down Your life for me
What can I do for You?
You have explained every mystery
What can I do for You?

Soon as a man is born, you know the sparks begin to fly
He gets wise in his own eyes and he's made to believe a lie
Who would deliver him from the death he's bound to die?
Well, You've done it all and there's no more anyone can
pretend to do

我能为您做什么？

您给了我一切
我能为您做什么？
您给我眼睛看见
我能为您做什么？

您解开我的绑索，使我内心焕然一新
填饱了一直遭拒绝的饥渴
您打开无人能关的门，开得如此
  宽阔
并且您拣选我成为少数
我能为您做什么？

您已经为我舍命
我能为您做什么？
您解释了每个奥秘
我能为您做什么？

人一出生，您知道火星即开始飞腾
他自视有智慧而此必信从虚谎
谁能将他从必死的死亡中解救？
哦，您做了一切，没人能够
  冒充

What can I do for You?

You have given all there is to give
What can I do for You?
You have given me life to live
How can I live for You?

I know all about poison, I know all about fiery darts
I don't care how rough the road is, show me where it starts
Whatever pleases You, tell it to my heart
Well, I don't deserve it but I sure did make it through
What can I do for You?

我能为您做什么？

您给了一切能给的
我能为您做什么？
您给我生命去活
我怎样才能为您而活？

我完全知晓毒气，完全知晓火箭
我不在乎路多崎岖，告诉我从哪儿开始
无论您意旨为何，但请明示我的心
哦，我配不上，但我一定有始有终
我能为您做什么？

SOLID ROCK

Well, I'm hangin' on to a solid rock
Made before the foundation of the world
And I won't let go, and I can't let go, won't let go
And I can't let go, won't let go and I can't let go no more

For me He was chastised, for me He was hated
For me He was rejected by a world that He created
Nations are angry, cursed are some
People are expecting a false peace to come

Well, I'm hangin' on to a solid rock
Made before the foundation of the world
And I won't let go and I can't let go, won't let go
And I can't let go, won't let go and I can't let go no more

It's the ways of the flesh to war against the spirit
Twenty-four hours a day you can feel it and you can hear it
Using all the devices under the sun
And He never give up 'til the battle's lost or won

Well, I'm hangin' on to a solid rock
Made before the foundation of the world

坚固磐石

哦，我紧紧抓住一块坚固磐石
它造于世界创造之先
所以我不会放手，也不能放手，不会放手
所以我不能放手，不会放手，我再不能放手

他为我受惩罚，为我被憎恨
他为了我被他创造的世界厌弃
外邦震怒，有人受到诅咒
人们期待着虚假的和平降临

哦，我紧紧抓住一块坚固磐石
它造于世界创造之先
所以我不会放手，也不能放手，不会放手
所以我不能放手，不会放手，我再不能放手

这就是肉身向灵魂开战的方式
一天二十四小时你都能感到，都能听到
用尽日光之下的一切手段
而他永不放弃，除非战争分出胜负

哦，我紧紧抓住一块坚固磐石
它造于世界创造之先

And I won't let go and I can't let go, won't let go

And I can't let go, won't let go and I can't let go no more

所以我不会放手，也不能放手，不会放手
所以我不能放手，不会放手，我再不能放手

PRESSING ON

Well I'm pressing on
Yes, I'm pressing on
Well I'm pressing on
To the higher calling of my Lord

Many try to stop me, shake me up in my mind
Say, "Prove to me that He is Lord, show me a sign"
What kind of sign they need when it all come from within
When what's lost has been found, what's to come has already
been?

Well I'm pressing on
Yes, I'm pressing on
Well I'm pressing on
To the higher calling of my Lord

Shake the dust off of your feet, don't look back
Nothing now can hold you down, nothing that you lack
Temptation's not an easy thing, Adam given the devil reign
Because he sinned I got no choice, it run in my vein

Well I'm pressing on

奋力前进

哦我在奋力前进
是的，我在奋力前进
哦我在奋力前进
向着我主更高的呼召

众人要阻止我，使我内心摇荡
说："给我证明他是主，显示神迹给我"
当一切都来自内心，他们要何种神迹
当丢失的已找回，将临的就已经
　来临吗？

哦我在奋力前进
是的，我在奋力前进
哦我在奋力前进
向着我主更高的呼召

跺去脚上的尘土，不可回头看
如今再没什么能阻止，你已完备无缺
诱惑并非易事，亚当其时被魔鬼辖制
因他的罪我别无选择，它流在我的血管里

哦我在奋力前进

Yes, I'm pressing on

Well I'm pressing on

To the higher calling of my Lord

是的，我在奋力前进
哦我在奋力前进
向着我主更高的呼召

IN THE GARDEN

When they came for Him in the garden, did they know?
When they came for Him in the garden, did they know?
Did they know He was the Son of God, did they know that He was Lord?
Did they hear when He told Peter, "Peter, put up your sword"?
When they came for Him in the garden, did they know?
When they came for Him in the garden, did they know?

When He spoke to them in the city, did they hear?
When He spoke to them in the city, did they hear?
Nicodemus came at night so he wouldn't be seen by men
Saying, "Master, tell me why a man must be born again"
When He spoke to them in the city, did they hear?
When He spoke to them in the city, did they hear?

When He healed the blind and crippled, did they see?
When He healed the blind and crippled, did they see?
When He said, "Pick up your bed and walk, why must you criticize?

在园中

当他们来园中[1]找他时，他们知道吗？
当他们来园中找他时，他们知道吗？
他们知道他是神的儿子，他们知道
　他是主吗？
当他对彼得说“彼得，收起你的刀”，他们听到了吗？
当他们来园中找他时，他们知道吗？
当他们来园中找他时，他们知道吗？

当他在城里对他们说话，他们听到了吗？
当他在城里对他们说话，他们听到了吗？
尼哥底母夜间前来，以免被人看见
他说：“主人，告诉我为什么人必须重生”
当他在城里对他们说话，他们听到了吗？
当他在城里对他们说话，他们听到了吗？

当他治好盲人和瘫痪者时，他们看到了吗？
当他治好盲人和瘫痪者时，他们看到了吗？
当他说：“拿着你的褥子走吧，为何你定要
　指摘？

---

[1] 园中，指客西马尼园，耶路撒冷的一个园子。《圣经》中，耶稣在这里被捕。

Same thing My Father do, I can do likewise"
When He healed the blind and crippled, did they see?
When He healed the blind and crippled, did they see?

Did they speak out against Him, did they dare?
Did they speak out against Him, did they dare?
The multitude wanted to make Him king, put a crown upon His
head
Why did He slip away to a quiet place instead?
Did they speak out against Him, did they dare?
Did they speak out against Him, did they dare?

When He rose from the dead, did they believe?
When He rose from the dead, did they believe?
He said, "All power is given to Me in heaven and on earth"
Did they know right then and there what the power was worth?
When He rose from the dead, did they believe?
When He rose from the dead, did they believe?

父所做的事，子也照样做”
当他治好盲人和瘫痪者时，他们看到了吗？
当他治好盲人和瘫痪者时，他们看到了吗？

他们公开反对他了吗，他们敢吗？
他们公开反对他了吗，他们敢吗？
众人要拥立他为王，将冠冕
　加于他
为何他反倒悄悄去了僻静地方呢？
他们公开反对他了吗，他们敢吗？
他们公开反对他了吗，他们敢吗？

当他从死人中复活，他们信吗？
当他从死人中复活，他们信吗？
他说：“天上地下所有的权柄都赐给我了”
当时当地他们知道这权柄的价值吗？
当他从死人中复活，他们信吗？
当他从死人中复活，他们信吗？

SAVING GRACE

If you find it in Your heart, can I be forgiven?
Guess I owe You some kind of apology
I've escaped death so many times, I know I'm only living
By the saving grace that's over me

By this time I'd-a thought I would be sleeping
In a pine box for all eternity
My faith keeps me alive, but I still be weeping
For the saving grace that's over me

Well, the death of life, then come the resurrection
Wherever I am welcome is where I'll be
I put all my confidence in Him, my sole protection
Is the saving grace that's over me

Well, the devil's shining light, it can be most blinding
But to search for love, that ain't no more than vanity
As I look around this world all that I'm finding
Is the saving grace that's over me

The wicked know no peace and you just can't fake it

救恩

若是你在您内心找到它，我能被宽恕吗?
我想我该向您致歉
死里逃生多少回，我知道我能活着
全靠加诸我身的救恩

到了这时候，我想我会
永世在一个松木箱中沉睡
是我的信仰让我活着，但我仍会哭泣
只为加诸我身的救恩

哦，生命死去，然后复活来临
无论我去往何方，我都会被接受
我全然信奉他，我唯一的庇护
就是加诸我身的救恩

哦，恶魔闪耀的光，可以是最耀眼的
但是去追寻爱吧，那些不过是虚荣
当我环顾这世界，我所找到的
都是加诸我身的救恩

恶人不得安宁，而你不能作伪

There's only one road and it leads to Calvary
It gets discouraging at times, but I know I'll make it
By the saving grace that's over me

这儿只有一条路，它通往髑髅地[1]
有时它令人灰心，但我知道我会做到
靠着加诸我身的救恩

[1] 髑髅地，耶稣的受难地。

ARE YOU READY?

Are you ready, are you ready?
Are you ready, are you ready?

Are you ready to meet Jesus?
Are you where you ought to be?
Will He know you when He sees you
Or will He say, "Depart from Me"?

Are you ready, hope you're ready
Am I ready, am I ready?
Am I ready, am I ready?

Am I ready to lay down my life for the brethren
And to take up my cross?
Have I surrendered to the will of God
Or am I still acting like the boss?

Am I ready, hope I'm ready

When destruction cometh swiftly

准备好了吗？[1]

准备好了吗，准备好了吗？
准备好了吗，准备好了吗？

准备好见耶稣了吗？
你在你该在的地方吗？
当他看到你，他会认识你吗
还是他会说“离开我去吧”？

准备好了吗，希望你准备好了
我准备好了吗，我准备好了吗？
我准备好了吗，我准备好了吗？

我准备好为弟兄舍命
背起我的十字架吗？
我顺服上帝的旨意了吗
还是依然表现得像个老大？

我准备好了吗？希望我准备好了

当毁灭疾速来临

---

[1] 本篇由杨盈盈校译。

And there's no time to say a fare-thee-well
Have you decided whether you want to be
In heaven or in hell?

Are you ready, are you ready?

Have you got some unfinished business?
Is there something holding you back?
Are you thinking for yourself
Or are you following the pack?

Are you ready, hope you're ready
Are you ready?

Are you ready for the judgment?
Are you ready for that terrible swift sword?
Are you ready for Armageddon?
Are you ready for the day of the Lord?

Are you ready, I hope you're ready

没时间去道永别
你决定好了吗
是上天堂还是下地狱？

准备好了吗，准备好了吗？

你还有未了的事吗？
还有事牵绊着你吗？
你还在为自己着想吗
还是你在随大流呢？

准备好了吗，希望你准备好了
准备好了吗？

准备好受审判了吗？
准备好领受那可怕的利剑了吗？
准备好面对哈米吉多顿[1]了吗？
准备好迎接主的日子了吗？

准备好了吗，我希望你准备好了

[1] 哈米吉多顿，指末日的善恶决战。

CITY OF GOLD

There is a City of Gold
Far from the rat race that eats at your soul
Far from the madness and the bars that hold
There is a City of Gold

There is a City of Light
Raised up in the heavens and the streets are bright
Glory to God—not by deeds or by might
There is a City of Light

There is a City of Love
Surrounded by stars and the powers above
Far from this world and the stuff dreams are made of
There is a City of Love

There is a City of Grace
You drink holy water in sanctified space
No one is afraid to show their face
In the City of Grace

黄金城

有一座黄金城
远离吞噬你灵魂的竞争
远离疯狂和路障
有一座黄金城

有一座光之城
高擎于天，街市明净
荣耀归于上帝——不靠行为和强力
有一座光之城

有一座爱之城
被众星和在天之力簇拥
远离这世界和构成梦的材料 [1]
有一座爱之城

有一座恩典城
你在圣所饮圣水
没人怕露出自己的脸
在这座恩典城

---

[1] 语出莎士比亚戏剧《暴风雨》第四幕第一场的台词："构成我们的料子也就是那梦幻的料子……"（朱生豪译文）

There is a City of Peace
Where all foul forms of destruction cease
Where the mighty have fallen and there are no police
There is a City of Peace

There is a City of Hope
Above the ravine on the green sunlit slope
All I need is an axe and a rope
To get to the City of Hope

I'm heading for the City of Gold
Before it's too late, before it gets too cold
Before I'm too tired, before I'm too old
I'm heading for the City of Gold

有一座平安城
一切毁坏之恶行都已终止
勇士退下，亦无警察
有一座平安城

有一座希望城
在幽谷上方，阳光照耀的绿坡上
我只需一把斧和一根绳
去往这希望城

我要去黄金城
在为时已晚之前，在天气大寒之前
在我太疲惫之前，在过于老迈之前
我要去黄金城

SHOT OF LOVE

SHOT OF LOVE
来一针爱

来一针爱

我的一颗心

耶稣名下所有

伦尼·布鲁斯

冲淡的爱

新郎还在圣坛前苦等

死人，死人

在夏季

烦恼

每一粒沙子

别说出去，这事就你知我知

附加歌词

加勒比海的风

需要个女人

安吉丽娜

你改变了我的生活

People tell me it's a sin
To know and see too much within
But I still believe she was my twin
I still can feel the sting (It was all and everything)
She was born in the Spring, (But I lost the ring)
But I was born too late,
Blame it on a Simple Twist of Fate

《来一针爱》是迪伦的第21张录音室专辑，发行于1981年8月12日。一般认为它是迪伦“基督三部曲”的最后一部，或淡出其福音主题的第一部。

这张专辑宗教、世俗主题杂糅，编曲配器植根于摇滚乐，而不像之前两部，有着浓厚的福音歌曲色彩。本张专辑同时收入了迪伦在录音期间的弃用作品。

迪伦自从开启其“救赎与重生”的新主题，就一直饱受评论界的严厉批评。评论家们普遍认为，那个挑战虚伪道德、撕开文化假面、刺穿政治黑幕的斗士变得怯弱、迂腐了，龟缩到宗教的陈腐教义中去了，成了20世纪60年代自由思想的反动力量。

“音乐的目的在于提升和激励精神，”迪伦在1983年接受《新音乐快递》采访时说道，“那些关心鲍勃·迪伦身在何处的人应该听听《来一针爱》。这是我最完美的歌曲。它从精神、音乐、爱情等各个层面定义了我身在何处，表明了我的同情心所在。所有的一切都在这首歌中。”

专辑第2首歌曲《我的一颗心》再次落脚在世俗和宗教的中间地带。这是一首轻快的得式－墨式（Tex-Mex）歌曲。从世俗的角度来看，它是迪伦多年来第一首情歌，但它的出发点在《旧约·耶利米书》17:9："人心比万物都诡诈，坏到极处，谁能识透呢？"

《伦尼·布鲁斯》是皈依基督教以来迪伦第一次在专辑中涉足世俗主题。布鲁斯是20世纪60年代的脱口秀演员、反主流文化人士，他对一切虚伪都嗤之以鼻，表演中常常将政治议题、种族问题、宗教信仰等都混为一场笑谈。尽管歌词是世俗的，但音乐锚定于福音钢琴坚定的韵律，迪伦罕有地为一位"颠覆人物"唱了一曲哀婉而肃然的颂歌。

《在夏季》展现了这一时期迪伦在思想上和艺术上的奇特。这首全专辑中似乎最为愉悦、轻松、宁静的歌曲，展现出在一个深情的回眸中，"有一种可爱的感觉，迪伦的口琴演奏像含羞草的香味一样悬在空中"（乐评人保罗·尼尔森语）。然而，迪伦所回望的事又都有宗教的含义，不仅仅有小时候邻居家窗口飘出的练琴声，"那个夏天"也是迪伦开始转变信仰的重要时刻。

支持和批评迪伦的人，都对《每一粒沙子》给予了赞美。这可能是迪伦最迷狂、最痛苦，也是最崇高、最神圣的歌曲。歌里有那么多的困惑，也有那么多的肯定；有那么多的脆弱，也有那么多的力量；有那么多的无奈，也有那么多的迷醉。这是迪伦在"基督教时期"创作出的可以与之前各个时期的代表作如《像一块滚石》《愚蠢的风》等媲美的佳作。

蒂姆·赖利（Tim Riley）将《每一粒沙子》描述为"一首与《答案在风中飘》处于同一直觉区域的祈祷文——你会发誓说这是一首流传千古的赞美诗"。摇滚评论家米洛·迈尔斯（Milo Miles）写道："这是迪伦10年来唯一的歌……在这首歌中，他比其他表演者更雄辩地印证了流行文化的悖论——传奇明星尤其必须相信比自己更伟大的理念。"

可以说，这张专辑有一部分内容，对批评者进行了反批评，一展他所擅长的"吵架模式"，迪伦对其"论敌"予以回击，对他们的虚伪、浅薄和愚蠢都进行了揭露和驳斥。

我们必须看到，迪伦在20世纪七八十年代向基督教义的转向有其深刻的思想动因。这种转向仍然是现实的，是迪伦面对时代问题、社会动荡、人生根本的进一步思考。专辑清晰地展现了迪伦此时思想的走向和精神所在的位置。

今天看来，迪伦的反击仍很有力，他所指出的问题指向了根本。比如，人们其实不接受"纯粹的爱"的真相，让人开眼；"烦恼"和苦难在人生境遇中的绝对性，呈示有力；对人类如"沙子"一般无所归依的处境，体验真切而深刻。而隐含着宗教意指的"新郎""安吉丽娜""加勒比海的风""我主与救主"等形象，都充满了迪伦的个人真实感受，富于文学感染力。

这张专辑的录音非常混乱，从1980年9月23日直到1981年6月7日，迪伦暴走加州（主要是洛杉矶），涉足至少6家录音室，前后用了3位制作人，进行了不下14场录音，才完成了这张将摇滚和福音结合在一起的唱片。

SHOT OF LOVE

I need a shot of love, I need a shot of love

Don't need a shot of heroin to kill my disease
Don't need a shot of turpentine, only bring me to my knees
Don't need a shot of codeine to help me to repent
Don't need a shot of whiskey, help me be president

I need a shot of love, I need a shot of love

Doctor, can you hear me? I need some Medicaid
I seen the kingdoms of the world and it's makin' me feel afraid
What I got ain't painful, it's just bound to kill me dead
Like the men that followed Jesus when they put a price upon
His head

I need a shot of love, I need a shot of love

I don't need no alibi when I'm spending time with you
I've heard all of them rumors and you have heard 'em too
Don't show me no picture show or give me no book to read

来一针爱[1]

我需要来一针爱，我需要来一针爱

不需要来针海洛因治愈我的病
不需要来管松节油，只会让我跪下
不需要来针可待因让我懊悔
不需要来杯威士忌，让我当上总统

我需要来一针爱，我需要来一针爱

医生，听到没有？我需要医疗救助
我看到世上的万国，这让我恐惧
我得的病不疼，只是要我的命
像那些追随耶稣的人，当他们定价了
　他的首级

我需要来一针爱，我需要来一针爱

我不需要不在场证据，既然我和你在一起
我听到的谣言你也全部听到了
不要给我放电影也不要给我书看

[1] 本篇为郝佳校译。

It don't satisfy the hurt inside nor the habit that it feeds

I need a shot of love, I need a shot of love

Why would I want to take your life?
You've only murdered my father, raped his wife
Tattooed my babies with a poison pen
Mocked my God, humiliated my friends

I need a shot of love, I need a shot of love

Don't wanna be with nobody tonight
Veronica not around nowhere, Mavis just ain't right
There's a man that hates me and he's swift, smooth and near
Am I supposed to set back and wait until he's here?

I need a shot of love, I need a shot of love

What makes the wind wanna blow tonight?
Don't even feel like crossing the street and my car ain't actin'
right
Called home, everybody seemed to have moved away
My conscience is beginning to bother me today

这治不了内伤也戒不掉毒瘾

我需要来一针爱，我需要来一针爱

为什么我非要取你性命？
你只是谋杀了我父亲，强奸了他妻子
用毒笔[1]给我的孩子文身
嘲笑我的神，羞辱我的朋友

我需要来一针爱，我需要来一针爱

今夜我不想和任何人在一起
维罗妮卡无影踪，梅维丝又不合适
有一个恨我的人，他敏捷、麻利就在附近
难道我该耽搁下去等他来吗？

我需要来一针爱，我需要来一针爱

今夜是什么让那风呼啸？
甚至不想过马路，我的车也
　不对劲
打个电话回家，所有人好像都搬走了
我的良心今天开始来骚扰我

---

[1] 毒笔，又指恶意中伤的匿名信。

I need a shot of love, I need a shot of love

I need a shot of love, I need a shot of love
If you're a doctor, I need a shot of love

我需要来一针爱，我需要来一针爱

我需要来一针爱，我需要来一针爱
如果你是医生，给我来一针爱吧

HEART OF MINE

Heart of mine be still
You can play with fire but you'll get the bill
Don't let her know
Don't let her know that you love her
Don't be a fool, don't be blind
Heart of mine

Heart of mine go back home
You got no reason to wander, you got no reason to roam
Don't let her see
Don't let her see that you need her
Don't put yourself over the line
Heart of mine

Heart of mine go back where you been
It'll only be trouble for you if you let her in
Don'tlet her hear
Don't let her hear you want her
Don't let her think you think she's fine
Heart of mine

Heart of mine you know that she'll never be true

我的一颗心

我的一颗心请你安静
你可以玩火但是你要付出代价
不要让她知道
不要让她知道你爱她
不要当傻瓜，不要睁眼瞎
我的一颗心啊

我的一颗心快回家
没理由再浪荡，没理由再溜达
不要让她看到
不要让她看出你需要她
不要让自己过线
我的一颗心啊

我的一颗心快回原来地方
这只会添乱如果你让她进来
不要让她听到
不要让她听到你想要她
不要让她觉得你觉得她很好
我的一颗心啊

我的一颗心你知道她从不真心

She'll only give to others the love that she's gotten from you
Don't let her know
Don't let her know where you're going
Don't untie the ties that bind
Heart of mine

Heart of mine so malicious and so full of guile
Give you an inch and you'll take a mile
Don't let yourself fall
Don't let yourself stumble
If you can't do the time, don't do the crime
Heart of mine

她只会把从你这儿弄到的爱给别人
不要让她知道
不要让她知道你要去哪儿
不要解开那系好的结
我的一颗心啊

我的一颗心如此恶毒充满狡诈
给你一寸你将进一里
不要让自己摔倒
不要让自己失足
如果你不愿坐牢，就不要犯罪
我的一颗心啊

PROPERTY OF JESUS

Go ahead and talk about him because he makes you doubt
Because he has denied himself the things that you can't live
without
Laugh at him behind his back just like the others do
Remind him of what he used to be when he comes walkin'
through

He's the property of Jesus
Resent him to the bone
You got something better
You've got a heart of stone

Stop your conversation when he passes on the street
Hope he falls upon himself, oh, won't that be sweet
Because he can't be exploited by superstition anymore
Because he can't be bribed or bought by the things that you
adore

He's the property of Jesus
Resent him to the bone
You got something better
You've got a heart of stone

耶稣名下所有

好吧谈谈他吧因为他让你有疑虑
因为他摒绝了你离了就活不了的
　东西
像其他人一样在背后嘲笑他吧
当他走过来，提醒他以前自己是
　什么样子

他是耶稣名下所有
你恨他恨得入骨
你有那更好的
你有那铁石之心

当他从街上走过时，你停下了话头
希望他自己摔一跤，啊，那该多美
因为他再不会被迷信利用
因为他不会被你们所崇拜的贿赂和
　收买

他是耶稣名下所有
你恨他恨得入骨
你有那更好的
你有那铁石之心

When the whip that's keeping you in line doesn't make him
jump
Say he's hard-of-hearin', say that he's a chump
Say he's out of step with reality as you try to test his nerve
Because he doesn't pay no tribute to the king that you serve

He's the property of Jesus
Resent him to the bone
You got something better
You've got a heart of stone

Say that he's a loser 'cause he got no common sense
Because he don't increase his worth at someone else's expense
Because he's not afraid of trying, 'cause he don't look at you
and smile
'Cause he doesn't tell you jokes or fairy tales, say he's got no
style

He's the property of Jesus
Resent him to the bone
You got something better
You've got a heart of stone

You can laugh at salvation, you can play Olympic games
You think that when you rest at last you'll go back from where

那使你规矩的鞭子却不会让他
　跳起
就说他笨耳朵，就说他木脑壳
你想测试他的胆量，说他脱离现实
因为他不向你伺候的国君进贡

他是耶稣名下所有
你恨他恨得入骨
你有那更好的
你有那铁石之心

说他是个失败者因为他毫无常识
因为他不为了利己而损人
因为他不怕尝试，因为他不看着
　你微笑
因为他不给你讲笑话和童话，就说他
　没有风度

他是耶稣名下所有
你恨他恨得入骨
你有那更好的
你有那铁石之心

你可以嘲笑那拯救，你可以参加奥运会
你认为当你长眠时你将回到你所来

you came
But you've picked up quite a story and you've changed since the womb
What happened to the real you, you've been captured but by whom?

He's the property of Jesus
Resent him to the bone
You got something better
You've got a heart of stone

之处
但你已有了好一段故事，从子宫开始就在
改变
那个真的你发生了什么，你究竟成了谁的
俘虏？

他是耶稣名下所有
你恨他恨得入骨
你有那更好的
你有那铁石之心

LENNY BRUCE

Lenny Bruce is dead but his ghost lives on and on
Never did get any Golden Globe award, never made it to
Synanon
He was an outlaw, that's for sure
More of an outlaw than you ever were
Lenny Bruce is gone but his spirit's livin' on and on

Maybe he had some problems, maybe some things that he
couldn't work out
But he sure was funny and he sure told the truth and he knew
what he was talkin' about
Never robbed any churches nor cut off any babies' heads
He just took the folks in high places and he shined a light in
their beds
He's on some other shore, he didn't wanna live anymore

伦尼·布鲁斯[1]

伦尼·布鲁斯死了但他的灵魂一直活着
从没得过金球奖，也没去过
　椴树村[2]
他是个不法之徒，确实如此
比你们做过的不法之徒更名副其实
伦尼·布鲁斯走了但他的精神一直活着

也许他有一些问题，也许有些事他无法
　解决
但是他确实有意思他确实讲了实话他知道
　他在说什么
从没抢劫过教堂也没砍过孩子的头
他只是揪住那些居于高处的人，投一束光在
　他们床上
他在别的海岸，他不想活了

---

[1] 伦尼·布鲁斯（1925—1966），美国喜剧演员、社会批评家、讽刺作家，因其表演破坏力太强，1964 年被判以“猥亵罪”。2003 年，时任纽约州长乔治·帕塔基就此致歉。

[2] 椴树村（Synanon），又译“希南农”，原为戒毒康复社区，1958 年在加州成立，有以“讲真话”为名的病患互相刺激的疗法，后演化为邪教组织，1991 年解体。

Lenny Bruce is dead but he didn't commit any crime
He just had the insight to rip off the lid before its time
I rode with him in a taxi once
Only for a mile and a half, seemed like it took a couple of
months
Lenny Bruce moved on and like the ones that killed him, gone

They said that he was sick 'cause he didn't play by the rules
He just showed the wise men of his day to be nothing more
than fools
They stamped him and they labeled him like they do with pants
and shirts
He fought a war on a battlefield where every victory hurts
Lenny Bruce was bad, he was the brother that you never had

伦尼·布鲁斯死了他什么恶都没作过
他只是敏锐地揭开了盖子，超前于那个时代
我有一次和他同乘一辆出租车
只一英里半的路，却像走了
　几个月
伦尼·布鲁斯继续前行，就像杀害他的那些人，死了

他们说他恶心因为他不按规矩出牌
其实他只是向他那个时代的智者表明他们
　不过是帮蠢货
他们给他盖章给他贴标签就像出厂的裤子和
　衬衣
他在一个战场上打了场战争那里每一场胜利都令人伤痛
伦尼·布鲁斯够坏，他是你从不曾拥有的兄弟

WATERED-DOWN LOVE

Love that's pure hopes all things
Believes all things, won't pull no strings
Won't sneak up into your room, tall, dark and handsome
Capture your heart and hold it for ransom

You don't want a love that's pure
You wanna drown love
You want a watered-down love

Love that's pure, it don't make no false claims
Intercedes for you 'stead of casting you blame
Will not deceive you or lead you into transgression
Won't write it up and make you sign a false confession

You don't want a love that's pure
You wanna drown love
You want a watered-down love

Love that's pure won't lead you astray
Won't hold you back, won't mess up your day

冲淡的爱[1]

纯粹的爱盼望一切
相信一切，不会暗中操纵
不会溜进卧室，高大、黝黑而英俊
俘获你的心，挟持它索要赎金

你不要纯粹的爱
你想把爱溺水里
你想要冲淡的爱

纯粹的爱从无不实之词
只会为你说情，而不是责备
不会蒙骗，引你上歧途
不会写出来让你签假供词

你不要纯粹的爱
你想把爱溺水里
你想要冲淡的爱

纯粹的爱不会让你迷路
不会拖后腿，不会搅乱你的日子

---

[1] 本篇由郝佳校译。

Won't pervert you, corrupt you with stupid wishes
It don't make you envious, it don't make you suspicious

You don't want a love that's pure
You wanna drown love
You want a watered-down love

Love that's pure ain't no accident
Always on time, is always content
An eternal flame, quietly burning
Never needs to be proud, restlessly yearning

You don't want a love that's pure
You wanna drown love
You want a watered-down love

不会以愚蠢的愿望腐蚀你，败坏你
不会让你嫉妒，让你疑神疑鬼

你不要纯粹的爱
你想把爱溺水里
你想要冲淡的爱

纯粹的爱不是什么意外
总是恰逢其时，总是令人满意
一支永恒的火焰，静静燃烧
从不需要张狂，辗转不安渴念

你不要纯粹的爱
你想把爱溺水里
你想要冲淡的爱

THE GROOM'S STILL WAITING AT THE ALTAR

Prayed in the ghetto with my face in the cement
Heard the last moan of a boxer, seen the massacre of the
innocent
Felt around for the light switch, became nauseated
She was walking down the hallway while the walls deteriorated

West of the Jordan, east of the Rock of Gibraltar
I see the turning of the page
Curtain risin' on a new age
See the groom still waitin' at the altar

Try to be pure at heart, they arrest you for robbery
Mistake your shyness for aloofness, your silence for snobbery
Got the message this morning, the one that was sent to me
About the madness of becomin' what one was never meant to
be

West of the Jordan, east of the Rock of Gibraltar
I see the burning of the stage
Curtain risin' on a new age

新郎还在圣坛前苦等[1]

我在贫民窟祈祷，脸埋在水泥里
听过拳击手最后的呻吟，看过无辜者
　被血洗
摸索着电灯开关，恶心欲呕
她走过门厅，那四壁已经恶化

约旦河以西，直布罗陀巨岩以东
我看到那页面翻过
新世纪的幕布升起
我看见新郎还在圣坛前苦等

想要达到心灵的纯净，他们以抢劫罪逮捕你
把羞怯误会成冷漠，把沉默误会成势利
今天早上收到给我的一条信息
关于那疯狂：成为从不想成为的
　那种人

约旦河以西，直布罗陀巨岩以东
我看见舞台烧起来
新世纪的幕布升起

---

[1] 基督教中，以新郎喻基督，以新娘喻教会。

See the groom still waitin' at the altar

Don't know what I can say about Claudette that wouldn't come
back to haunt me
Finally had to give her up 'bout the time she began to want me
But I know God has mercy on them who are slandered and
humiliated
I'd a-done anything for that woman if she didn't make me feel
so obligated

West of the Jordan, east of the Rock of Gibraltar
I see the burning of the cage
Curtain risin' on a new stage
See the groom still waitin' at the altar

Put your hand on my head, baby, do I have a temperature?
I see people who are supposed to know better standin' around
like furniture
There's a wall between you and what you want and you got to
leap it
Tonight you got the power to take it, tomorrow you won't have
the power to keep it

West of the Jordan, east of the Rock of Gibraltar
I see the burning of the stage
Curtain risin' on a new age

我看见新郎还在圣坛前苦等

不知我该怎么说克劳黛特，她不会再回来
　纠缠我了
终于必须放弃她，大概在她开始想要我时
但是我知道上帝垂怜受诽谤和
　受羞辱的人
为那女人我什么都愿做，要是她不曾让
　我深感负有义务

约旦河以西，直布罗陀巨岩以东
我看见牢房烧起来
新世纪的幕布升起
我看见新郎还在圣坛前苦等

摸摸我的头，宝贝，我是不是在发烧？
我看见那些本该更明白的人像家具般
　干站着
在你和你想要的东西之间有一堵墙
　你要跃过
今夜你有了力量去得到，明天你不会
　还有力量拥有

约旦河以西，直布罗陀巨岩以东
我看见舞台烧起来
新世纪的幕布升起

See the groom still waitin' at the altar

Cities on fire, phones out of order
They're killing nuns and soldiers, there's fighting on the border
What can I say about Claudette? Ain't seen her since January
She could be respectfully married or running a whorehouse in
Buenos Aires

West of the Jordan, east of the Rock of Gibraltar
I see the burning of the stage
Curtain risin' on a new age
See the groom still waitin' at the altar

我看见新郎还在圣坛前苦等

城市着火，电话失灵
他们在屠杀修女和士兵，边境战争爆发
我该怎么说克劳黛特？一月以来我就没见过她
她也许已经体面地结婚了，也许在布宜诺斯艾利斯
　开窑子

约旦河以西，直布罗陀巨岩以东
我看见舞台烧起来
新世纪的幕布升起
我看见新郎还在圣坛前苦等

DEAD MAN, DEAD MAN

Uttering idle words from a reprobate mind
Clinging to strange promises, dying on the vine
Never bein' able to separate the good from the bad
Ooh, I can't stand it, I can't stand it
It's makin' me feel so sad

Dead man, dead man
When will you arise?
Cobwebs in your mind
Dust upon your eyes

Satan got you by the heel, there's a bird's nest in your hair
Do you have any faith at all? Do you have any love to share?
The way that you hold your head, cursin' God with every move
Ooh, I can't stand it, I can't stand it
What are you tryin' to prove?

Dead man, dead man
When will you arise?
Cobwebs in your mind
Dust upon your eyes

死人，死人

空洞无聊的话来自邪僻之心
执着于奇怪的允诺，还没结果就蔫在藤上
永远不能区分好与坏
啊，我再不能忍受，我再不能忍受
这让我多么悲伤

死人，死人
你何时复活？
你的心结满蛛网
你的眼睛满是灰尘

撒旦捉着你脚后跟，你的发丛筑了鸟窝
你到底有没有信仰？你有没有爱要分享？
你拧着头的样子，每个动作都是在诅咒上帝
啊，我再不能忍受，我再不能忍受
你想要证明什么？

死人，死人
你何时复活？
你的心结满蛛网
你的眼睛满是灰尘

The glamour and the bright lights and the politics of sin
The ghetto that you build for me is the one you end up in
The race of the engine that overrules your heart
Ooh, I can't stand it, I can't stand it
Pretending that you're so smart

Dead man, dead man
When will you arise?
Cobwebs in your mind
Dust upon your eyes

What are you tryin' to overpower me with, the doctrine or the
  gun?
My back is already to the wall, where can I run?
The tuxedo that you're wearin', the flower in your lapel
Ooh, I can't stand it, I can't stand it
You wanna take me down to hell

Dead man, dead man
When will you arise?
Cobwebs in your mind
Dust upon your eyes

诱惑、花花世界和罪恶的政治
你为我造的贫民窟也是你最后的栖身之地
引擎空转支配了你的心
啊，我再不能忍受，我再不能忍受
假装你是多么聪明

死人，死人
你何时复活？
你的心结满蛛网
你的眼睛满是灰尘

你想用什么制服我，教义
　还是枪？
我的背已抵着墙，我还能逃到哪儿去？
你穿着小礼服，翻领上簪着花
啊，我再不能忍受，我再不能忍受
你想把我拖进地狱

死人，死人
你何时复活？
你的心结满蛛网
你的眼睛满是灰尘

IN THE SUMMERTIME

I was in your presence for an hour or so
Or was it a day? I truly don't know
Where the sun never set, where the trees hung low
By that soft and shining sea
Did you respect me for what I did
Or for what I didn't do, or for keeping it hid?
Did I lose my mind when I tried to get rid
Of everything you see?

In the summertime, ah in the summertime
In the summertime, when you were with me

I got the heart and you got the blood
We cut through iron and we cut through mud
Then came the warnin' that was before the flood
That set everybody free
Fools they made a mock of sin
Our loyalty they tried to win
But you were closer to me than my next of kin
When they didn't want to know or see

在夏季[1]

我在你面前已经一小时左右
还是已有一天？我真的不知道
太阳一直未落，而树枝低垂
在那柔和而灿烂的大海边
你是否钦敬我的所为
或者为我不做的，为我所隐藏的？
我是否已失去理智，当我试图摆脱
你看到的一切？

在夏季，啊在夏季
在夏季，当你和我在一起

我有这颗心而你有这热血
我们穿过了铁幕我们穿过了泥泞
然后传来了警告洪水要来了
洪水让所有人都获得自由
愚妄人犯罪以为戏耍
他们试图赢得我们的忠诚
但是你比我的亲人更亲近
当他们不想知道也不想看到

[1] 本篇由郝佳校译。

In the summertime, ah in the summertime
In the summertime when you were with me

Strangers, they meddled in our affairs
Poverty and shame was theirs
But all that sufferin' was not to be compared
With the glory that is to be
And I'm still carrying the gift you gave
It's a part of me now, it's been cherished and saved
It'll be with me unto the grave
And then unto eternity

In the summertime, ah in the summertime
In the summertime when you were with me

在夏季，啊在夏季
在夏季，当你和我在一起

异乡人插手着我们的事
贫穷和耻辱是他们的
而所有的苦楚都不能与
将要到来的荣耀比拟
我依然带着你给的礼物
它现在成了我的一部分，受到珍爱和保存
将随我到坟墓
随我到永恒

在夏季，啊在夏季
在夏季，当你和我在一起

TROUBLE

Trouble in the city, trouble in the farm
You got your rabbit's foot, you got your good-luck charm
But they can't help you none when there's trouble

Trouble
Trouble, trouble, trouble
Nothin' but trouble

Trouble in the water, trouble in the air
Go all the way to the other side of the world, you'll find trouble
there
Revolution even ain't no solution for trouble

Trouble
Trouble, trouble, trouble
Nothin' but trouble

Drought and starvation, packaging of the soul
Persecution, execution, governments out of control

烦恼

在城市烦恼，在农场烦恼
你有了幸运符，你有了兔子脚[1]
但是它们无济于事当你有了烦恼

烦恼
烦恼，烦恼，烦恼
别无他物只有烦恼

在水里烦恼，在空中烦恼
一路走到世界另一侧，你还是
　会烦恼
甚至革命也不能解决烦恼

烦恼
烦恼，烦恼，烦恼
别无他物只有烦恼

干旱和饥荒，把灵魂打包
迫害，行刑，失控的政府

---

[1] 在一些文化中，兔子脚被认为能带来好运。

You can see the writing on the wall inviting trouble

Trouble
Trouble, trouble, trouble
Nothin' but trouble

Put your ear to the train tracks, put your ear to the ground
You ever feel like you're never alone even when there's nobody
else around?
Since the beginning of the universe man's been cursed by
trouble

Trouble
Trouble, trouble, trouble
Nothin' but trouble

Nightclubs of the broken-hearted, stadiums of the damned
Legislature, perverted nature, doors that are rudely slammed
Look into infinity, all you see is trouble

Trouble
Trouble, trouble, trouble
Nothin' but trouble

你可以看到墙上的字[1]在邀请烦恼

烦恼
烦恼，烦恼，烦恼
别无他物只有烦恼

把耳朵贴近铁轨，把耳朵贴近地面
你是否觉得你从不是一个人即使周围
　空无一人？
从宇宙之初人就受了诅咒，被
　烦恼

烦恼
烦恼，烦恼，烦恼
别无他物只有烦恼

伤心人夜总会，受诅咒者的体育场
立法机关，变态人性，粗暴摔上的门
洞穿那无穷，所见尽是烦恼

烦恼
烦恼，烦恼，烦恼
别无他物只有烦恼

---

[1] “墙上的字”，指凶兆。

EVERY GRAIN OF SAND

In the time of my confession, in the hour of my deepest need
When the pool of tears beneath my feet flood every newborn
  seed
There's a dyin' voice within me reaching out somewhere
Toiling in the danger and in the morals of despair

Don't have the inclination to look back on any mistake
Like Cain, I now behold this chain of events that I must break
In the fury of the moment I can see the Master's hand
In every leaf that trembles, in every grain of sand

Oh, the flowers of indulgence and the weeds of yesteryear
Like criminals, they have choked the breath of conscience and
  good cheer
The sun beat down upon the steps of time to light the way
To ease the pain of idleness and the memory of decay

I gaze into the doorway of temptation's angry flame
And every time I pass that way I always hear my name

每一粒沙子 [1]

在我忏悔时，在我最深切渴求时
我脚下的泪池淹没了每一粒新生的
　种子
体内升起一个垂死的声音它向某处伸展着
爬行在危险中爬行在绝望的道德里

不要有任何回顾错误的倾向
就像是该隐 [2]，我现在才看到这条必须打破的事件链
在这一刻的暴怒中我能看见主人的手
在每一片战栗的叶子上，在每一粒沙子里

啊，沉溺的花和往昔的野草
就像是罪犯，扼住了良知和欢乐的
　呼吸
太阳打在时间的台阶上，照亮道路
舒缓那百无聊赖的痛苦和腐朽的记忆

我盯着诱惑的怒火之门廊
每一次当我走过，我都听到自己的名字

---

[1] 本篇由郝佳校译。

[2] 该隐，《圣经》中亚当和夏娃的儿子，第一个杀人者。

Then onward in my journey I come to understand
That every hair is numbered like every grain of sand

I have gone from rags to riches in the sorrow of the night
In the violence of a summer's dream, in the chill of a wintry light
In the bitter dance of loneliness fading into space
In the broken mirror of innocence on each forgotten face

I hear the ancient footsteps like the motion of the sea
Sometimes I turn, there's someone there, other times it's only me
I am hanging in the balance of the reality of man
Like every sparrow falling, like every grain of sand

继续向前走，我渐渐得以明白
每一根头发都被数过了，就像每一粒沙子

我从赤贫变成巨富，在夜的悲哀中
在夏之梦的暴力中，在冬之光的
　寒意中
在寂寞遁空的苦涩舞蹈中
在映着每一张遗忘面孔的天真之碎镜中

我听到那远古的脚步就像海洋的运动
我转过身去，有时有人在那儿，有时
　只有我自己
我对人的本质仍摇摆不定
像是每一只坠落的麻雀，像是每一粒沙子

LET'S KEEP IT BETWEEN US

Let's keep it between us
These people meddlin' in our affairs, they're not our friends
Let's keep it between us
Before doors close and our togetherness comes to an end
They'll turn you against me and me against you
'Til we don't know who to trust
Oh, darlin', can we keep it between us?

Let's keep it between us
We've been through too much tough times that they never
  shared
They've had nothing to say to us before
Now all of a sudden it's as if they've always cared
All we need is honesty
A little humility and trust
Oh, darlin', can we keep it between us?

I know we're not perfect
Then again, neither are they
They act like we got to live for them
As if there just ain't no other way
And it's makin' me kind of tired

别说出去，这事就你知我知

别说出去，这事就你知我知
这些人插手我们的事，他们不在我们这边
别说出去，这事就你知我知
在所有门关上前，在你我散伙前
他们要拉你反对我，拉我反对你
直到我们不知道该信谁
啊亲爱的，能否别说出去，这事就你知我知？

别说出去，这事就你知我知
我们共度了这许多艰难时刻他们
　哪分担过
以前他们对我们什么都不说
现在却突然好像他们一直都很关切
我们需要的只是诚实
和一点点谦逊及信任
啊亲爱的，能否别说出去，这事就你知我知？

我知道我们不完美
但话说回来，他们也不完美
他们表现得好像我们必须为他们而活
好像就没别的法子
这让人有点儿累啊

Can we just lay back for a moment
Before we wake up and find ourselves in a daze that's got us
out of our minds?
There must be something we're overlooking here
We better drop down now and get back behind the lines
There's some things not fit for human ears
Some things don't need to be discussed
Oh, darlin', can we keep it between us?

They'll tell you one thing and me another
'Til we don't know who to trust
Oh, darlin', can we keep it between us?

Let's keep it between us
Before it all snaps and goes too far
If we can't deal with this by ourselves
Tell me we ain't worse off than they think we are
Backseat drivers don't know the feel of the wheel
But they sure know how to make a fuss
Oh, darlin', can we keep it between us?

Can we keep it between us?

我们能不能倒回去一点儿
回到发觉自己失去理智的
　恍惚之前？
在这里想必我们忽略了什么
我们最好现在就放下并退回线后
有些事人耳听不得
有些事不需要讨论
啊亲爱的，能否别说出去，这事就你知我知？

他们会告诉你这样而告诉我那样
直到我们不知道该信谁
啊亲爱的，能否别说出去，这事就你知我知？

别说出去，这事就你知我知
在事情完全破裂、无法挽回之前
如果这事我们自己搞不定
至少你我并不比他们认为的更糟
坐后座指挥的人怎知道方向盘的感觉
但是他们当然懂得如何大惊小怪
啊亲爱的，能否别说出去，这事就你知我知？

能否别说出去，这事就你知我知？

CARIBBEAN WIND

She was the rose of Sharon from paradise lost
From the city of seven hills near the place of the cross
I was playing a show in Miami in the theater of divine comedy
Told about Jesus, told about the rain
She told me about the jungle where her brothers were slain
By a man who danced on the roof of the embassy

Was she a child or a woman, I can't say which
From one to another she could easily switch
We went into the wall to where the long arm of the law could
  not reach
Could I been used and played as a pawn?
It certainly was possible as the gay night wore on
Where men bathed in perfume and celebrated free speech

And them Caribbean winds still blow from Nassau to Mexico
Fanning the flames in the furnace of desire
And them distant ships of liberty on them iron waves so bold

加勒比海的风[1]

她是失乐园的沙仑玫瑰
来自十字架圣地附近的七丘之城[2]
我在迈阿密的神曲剧院演出
她跟我说起耶稣，说起雨
还说起她的兄弟们遇害的丛林
凶手是一个在大使馆屋顶跳舞的人

她是小孩还是女人？我说不清
从一个到另一个她切换得轻松
我们进入墙内法律的长臂无法
　触及
我会被人当棋子利用和玩弄吗？
这当然有可能，愉快的夜慢慢过去
人们一边在香水中沐浴，一边赞颂着言论自由

而加勒比海的风还在从拿骚[3]吹到墨西哥
煽动那欲望火炉里的火
而远方的自由船舶在铁浪上是这样

---

[1] 本篇由郝佳、杨盈盈校译。

[2] 七丘之城（the city of seven hills），常指罗马，此处可能为耶路撒冷。

[3] 拿骚，巴哈马首都。

and free
Bringing everything that's near to me nearer to the fire

She looked into my soul through the clothes that I wore
She said, "We got a mutual friend over by the door
And you know he's got our best interest in mind"
He was well connected but her heart was a snare
And she had left him to die in there
There were payments due and he was a little behind

The cry of the peacock, flies buzz my head
Ceiling fan broken, there's a heat in my bed
Street band playing "Nearer My God to Thee"
We met at the steeple where the mission bells ring
She said, "I know what you're thinking, but there ain't a thing
You can do about it, so let us just agree to agree"

And them Caribbean winds still blow from Nassau to Mexico
Fanning the flames in the furnace of desire
And them distant ships of liberty on them iron waves so bold
and free
Bringing everything that's near to me nearer to the fire

　英勇不羁
令我近处的一切更接近火焰

她的目光穿过外衣透射进我的灵魂
她说："门那边有咱俩都认识的一个朋友
你知道吧，他总是在惦记着我们的最大利益"
他交际很广但她的心是个陷阱
她让他死在了那儿
有一些应付账款而他没及时付清

孔雀的叫声，苍蝇在我头上嗡嗡嗡
吊扇坏了，我的床热气腾腾
街头乐队在表演着《更近我主》[1]
我们约在教堂尖顶那儿钟声长鸣
她说："我知道你在想什么，但其实做什么都
无济于事，所以让我们同意我们的同意吧"

而加勒比海的风还在从拿骚吹到墨西哥
煽动那欲望火炉里的火
而远方的自由船舶在铁浪上是这样
　英勇不羁
令我近处的一切更接近火焰

---

[1] 《更近我主》（"Nearer My God to Thee"），英国诗人萨拉·亚当斯创作的赞美诗，后谱成著名小提琴曲。泰坦尼克号沉没前，船上乐队曾演奏，给蒙难者以激励。

Atlantic City by the cold grey sea
I hear a voice crying, "Daddy," I always think it's for me
But it's only the silence in the buttermilk hills that call
Every new messenger brings evil report
'Bout armies on the march and time that is short
And famines and earthquakes and hatred written upon walls

Would I have married her? I don't know, I suppose
She had bells in her braids and they hung to her toes
But I kept hearing my name and had to be movin' on
I saw screws break loose, saw the devil pound tin
I saw a house in the country being torn from within
I heard my ancestors calling from the land far beyond

And them Caribbean winds still blow from Nassau to Mexico
Fanning the flames in the furnace of desire
And them distant ships of liberty on them iron waves so bold
 and free
Bringing everything that's near to me nearer to the fire

阴冷灰暗的大海边的大西洋城
我听到一个声音喊“爸爸”，我总以为是在叫我
但这只是酪乳山的寂静在呼唤
每一个新信使都带来坏消息
关于行军中的军队和所剩无几的时间
关于饥荒和地震和写在墙上的仇恨

我会娶她吗？我不知道，本该娶吧
她在发辫上挂满铃铛，一直垂向了足尖
但我一直听见我的名字，必须继续向前
我看见螺丝松了，看见魔鬼一磅装罐头[1]
看见乡下一栋房子从内部被扯烂
听见我的祖先在遥远的国度呼唤

而加勒比海的风还在从拿骚吹到墨西哥
煽动那欲望火炉里的火
而远方的自由船舶在铁浪上是这样
　英勇不羁
令我近处的一切更接近火焰

---

[1] 魔鬼一磅装罐头，指佩科拉石棉耐火水泥。1899 年佩科拉公司注册了魔鬼商标。

NEED A WOMAN

It's been raining in the trenches all day long, dripping down to
my clothes
My patience is wearing thin, got a fire inside my nose
Searching for the truth the way God designed it
The truth is I might drown before I find it

Well I need a woman, yes I do
Need a woman, yes I do
Someone who can see me as I am
Somebody who just don't give a damn
And I want you to be that woman every night
Be that woman

I've had my eyes on you baby for about five long years
You probably don't know me at all, but I have seen your
laughter and tears
Now you don't frighten me, my heart is jumping
And you look like it wouldn't hurt you none to have a man who
could give ya something

需要个女人[1]

沟里终日在下雨，雨水滴进
　衣服
我的耐性在消退，鼻子里有团火
我寻找着真理，方式乃上帝设计
真理就是还没找到它，我可能已被淹死

好吧我需要个女人，是的我要
需要个女人，是的我要
一个能看懂我的人
一个根本不在乎的人
而我多想你就是那个女人，每一夜
你就是那个女人

我一直盯着你宝贝，差不多五年了
你可能压根儿不认识我，但是我见过
　你的笑和泪水
好啦别吓我，我的心在跳
看来有个能给你点什么的人，不会
　对你有害处

---

[1] 本篇由郝佳、杨盈盈校译。

Well I need a woman, oh don't I
Need a woman, bring it home safe at last
Seen you turn the corner, seen your boot heels spark
Seen you in the daylight, and watched you in the dark
And I want you to be that woman, all right
Be that woman every night

Well, if you believe in something long enough you just
naturally come to think it's true
There ain't no wall you can't cross over, ain't no fire you can't
walk through
Well, believing is all right, just don't let the wrong people
know what it's all about
They might put the evil eye on you, use their hidden powers to
try to turn you out

Well I need a woman, just to be my queen
Need a woman, know what I mean?

好吧我需要个女人，啊不是吗
需要个女人，让家里最终平平安安
看见你转过拐角，看见你靴跟的闪光
看见你在日光中，注视你在黑暗中
而我多想你就是那个女人，好吗
你就是那个女人每夜每夜

好吧，假如你信某事够久，你自然
　就会当真
没你越不过的墙，没你
　穿不过的火
好吧，相信没错，只是别让不对的人
　知道这一切
他们会以恶眼相看，用暗力将你
　驱逐

好吧我需要个女人，让她做我的女王
需要个女人，明白我意思吧？

ANGELINA

Well, it's always been my nature to take chances
My right hand drawing back while my left hand advances
Where the current is strong and the monkey dances
To the tune of a concertina

Blood dryin' in my yellow hair as I go from shore to shore
I know what it is that has drawn me to your door
But whatever it could be, makes me think you've seen me
before
Angelina

Oh, Angelina. Oh, Angelina

His eyes were two slits that would make a snake proud
With a face that any painter would paint as he walked through
the crowd
Worshipping a god with the body of a woman well endowed
And the head of a hyena

Do I need your permission to turn the other cheek?
If you can read my mind, why must I speak?
No, I have heard nothing about the man that you seek

安吉丽娜

哦，冒险一直是我的天性
右手缩回，左手却伸出去
在水流湍急的地方还有猴子跳舞
伴着那六角风琴奏出的曲子

我黄头发里的血干了，当我从一个海岸走到另一个
我知道是什么吸引我到你门前
但不管它是什么吧，它让我觉得你以前
　见过我
安吉丽娜

啊，安吉丽娜。啊，安吉丽娜

他的眼睛是两道能让蛇骄傲的裂缝
一张脸画家们都想画当他举步穿过
　人群
敬奉一个神，有着大胸女人的身躯
和鬣狗的头

我需要你的允许才能转过另一边脸吗？
如果你能读懂我的心，我为什么还要说话？
不，我没有听说过你要找的那个人

Angelina

Oh, Angelina. Oh, Angelina

In the valley of the giants where the stars and stripes explode
The peaches they were sweet and the milk and honey flowed
I was only following instructions when the judge sent me down
the road
With your subpoena

When you cease to exist, then who will you blame
I've tried my best to love you but I cannot play this game
Your best friend and my worst enemy is one and the same
Angelina

Oh, Angelina. Oh, Angelina

There's a black Mercedes rollin' through the combat zone
Your servants are half dead, you're down to the bone
Tell me, tall men, where would you like to be overthrown
Maybe down in Jerusalem or Argentina?

安吉丽娜

啊，安吉丽娜。啊，安吉丽娜

巨人谷[1]的星条旗激增
那儿桃子很甜，奶与蜜四处流
法官派我上路我谨遵
　指令
身上带着你的传票

当你不复存在，那时你会怪谁
我已尽全力爱你但我不会玩这个游戏
你最好的朋友和我最坏的敌人是同一人
安吉丽娜

啊，安吉丽娜。啊，安吉丽娜

一辆黑色梅赛德斯驶过战区
你的仆人们半死不活，你伤得露出骨头
告诉我，大个子，你们打算到哪儿覆灭
耶路撒冷，还是阿根廷？[2]

---

[1] 皮特·B. 凯恩（Peter B. Kyne）于1918年创作了一部名为《巨人谷》的小说，讲述了加利福尼亚的诚实磨坊主比尔·卡迪根和前来伐木的外来贪婪商人之间的较量，据说迪伦对此部小说颇为欣赏。

[2] "耶路撒冷，还是阿根廷？"二战结束后，很多纳粹分子躲到了阿根廷，包括后来在耶路撒冷受审的艾希曼。

She was stolen from her mother when she was three days old
Now her vengeance has been satisfied and her possessions
have been sold
He's surrounded by God's angels and she's wearin' a blindfold
And so are you, Angelina

Oh, Angelina. Oh, Angelina

I see pieces of men marching, trying to take heaven by force
I can see the unknown rider, I can see the pale white horse
In God's truth tell me what you want and you'll have it of
course
Just step into the arena

Beat a path of retreat up them spiral staircases
Pass the tree of smoke, pass the angel with four faces
Begging God for mercy and weepin' in unholy places
Angelina

Oh, Angelina. Oh, Angelina

她出生才三天就被从母亲身边偷走
现在她心满意足报了仇，她的财产
　已经出售
他被上帝的天使包围而她戴着眼罩
你也是这样，安吉丽娜

啊，安吉丽娜。啊，安吉丽娜

我看见一片人海在进军，试图用武力占领天堂
我能看见那个不明身份的骑士，我能看见那匹苍白色的马
以上帝的真理告诉我你要什么，然后当然你将
　拥有
来，请下场子吧

沿旋转楼梯而上，开出一条撤退之路
经过烟云之树，经过那四脸天使[1]
乞求上帝怜悯，并在不洁之地哭泣
安吉丽娜

啊，安吉丽娜。啊，安吉丽娜

---

[1] 四脸天使（the angel with four faces），《旧约·以西结书》中提到以西结所见异象中，有四张脸孔的活物，四张脸孔分别是人脸、狮子脸、牛脸和鹰脸。

YOU CHANGED MY LIFE

I was listening to the voices of death on parade
Singing about conspiracy, wanted me to be afraid
Working for a system I couldn't understand or trust
Suffered ridicule and wanting to give it all up in disgust

But you changed my life
Came along in a time of strife
In hunger and need, you made my heart bleed
You changed my life

Talk about salvation, people suddenly get tired
They got a million things to do, they're all so inspired
You do the work of the devil, you got a million friends
They'll be there when you got something, they'll take it all in
the end

But you changed my life
Came along in a time of strife
I was under the gun, clouds blocking the sun
You changed my life

Well, the nature of man is to beg and to steal

你改变了我的生活

我在听死亡游行的声音
它唱着阴谋，想让我恐惧
为我不能理解和相信的体制工作
受奚落折磨，渴望在厌恶中彻底放弃

但是你改变了我的生活
在冲突四起的时候不期而至
怀着饥渴和需要，你让我的心流血
你改变了我的生活

谈论着拯救，人们突然厌倦
他们有一百万件事要做，他们全都欢欣鼓舞
你在行魔鬼之所为，你有一百万个朋友
当你有了收获他们全来了，最后他们会把它
　全收走

但是你改变了我的生活
在冲突四起的时候不期而至
我被枪指着，乌云挡住太阳
你改变了我的生活

哦，人的本性就是乞和偷

I do it myself, it's not so unreal
The call of the wild is forever at my door
Wants me to fly like an eagle while being chained to the floor

But you changed my life
Came along in a time of strife
From silver and gold to what man cannot hold
You changed my life

I was eating with the pigs off a fancy tray
I was told I was looking good and to have a nice day
It all seemed so proper, it all seemed so elite
Eating that absolute garbage while being so discreet

But you changed my life
Came along in a time of strife
From silver and gold to what man cannot hold
You changed my life

You were glowing in the sun while being peaceably calm
While orphans of man danced to the beat of the palm
Your eyes were on fire, your feet were of brass
In the world you had made they made you an outcast

You changed my life
Came along in a time of strife

我自己干，它不是那么不真实
野性的呼唤永远在拍打我的门
想让我像雄鹰翱翔而我其实是被铸在地上

但是你改变了我的生活
在冲突四起的时候不期而至
从银和金到人无法控制的
你改变了我的生活

我和猪一起从花式盘中吃饭
人们告诉我我很好，并祝我度过美好一天
一切似乎很得体，一切似乎很高档
吃着那绝对的垃圾举止如此矜持

但是你改变了我的生活
在冲突四起的时候不期而至
从银和金到人无法控制的
你改变了我的生活

你在阳光中容光焕发同时也平静宁和
而人类的孤儿应着那单掌的节拍在跳舞
你的眼目如火，你的脚是铜做的
在你创造的世界中，他们抛弃了你

你改变了我的生活
在冲突四起的时候不期而至

From silver and gold to what man cannot hold
You changed my life

There was someone in my body that I could hardly see
Invading my privacy making my decisions for me
Holding me back, not letting me stand
Making me feel like a stranger in a strange land

But you changed my life
Came along in a time of strife
You come down the line, gave me a new mind
You changed my life

My Lord and my Savior, my companion, my friend
Heart fixer, mind regulator, true to the end
My creator, my comforter, my cause for joy
What the world is set against but will never destroy

You changed my life
Came along in a time of strife
You came in like the wind, like Errol Flynn
You changed my life

从银和金到人无法控制的
你改变了我的生活

在我身体里有个我几乎看不见的人
侵入我的隐私，帮我做决定
拽住我，不让我站起来
让我觉得自己像在外邦做了寄居的

但是你改变了我的生活
在冲突四起的时候不期而至
你出现了，给我一个新心灵
你改变了我的生活

我主与救主，我的伴侣，我的朋友
他又是修复心灵的人，监管意志的人，最终的真实
我的造物主，我的慰藉者，我快乐的根由
那个世界所反对却永不能摧毁的

你改变了我的生活
在冲突四起的时候不期而至
你像风一样进来了，像埃罗尔 · 弗林[1]
你改变了我的生活

---

[1] 埃罗尔·弗林（1909—1959），美国演员，以饰演侠盗著称，主演过《罗宾汉历险记》（1938）等，一生放纵不羁、贪酒好色，有名言“我爱威士忌年久、女人年轻”。